THINGS TO DO NOW THAT YOU'RE...A GRANDPARENT

things to do now

AMY GOYER   Illustrations by Robyn Neild

that you're...
a grandparent

spruce

contents

introduction

It's finally happened! You are, at long last, a grandparent! Why do so many grandparents say if they had known it would be so great, they would have become a grandparent first? Because it's one of the most unique, enjoyable, and rewarding roles you will ever play—most grandparents love the freedom of more choices and less responsibility when it comes to their relationships with grandchildren. The joys of sharing family history, hobbies, travels, and just having fun with your grandchildren will fill your life with a renewed vitality and vigor.

Looking for creative new ways to connect with grandkids and support their parents? You're in the right place. Your instincts will kick in and you will probably be quite surprised at the things you'll do with those precious children—

activities you never thought you'd be doing! Grandchildren will motivate you to try new things and to be the absolute best you can be.

Just like any role in life, there will be challenges as well as joys—from baby equipment and discipline to caregiving, family relationships, technology, and simply trying to keep energetic children and moody teens occupied. And you can bet that some things have changed since you raised your children. Not to worry! Including 600 ideas, tips, and experiences to help you build strong relationships with your grandchildren of all ages, *Things to do now that you're…a GRANDPARENT* will help you navigate through this new, fulfiling world of being their very special, loving grandparent!

straight from the heart

Tell your grandchildren you love them every chance you get. Your unconditional love is magic to a grandchild, and that's what they will remember about you the most.

Let your grandchildren be themselves. They are wonderful, unique people from the time they are born, and you will always love them for whom they are.

Show up—just being there for your grandchildren's school events, performances, games, and matches will tell them how important they are to you.

Let your grandchildren know you're not perfect, and it's OK that they aren't either.

Your grandchildren will usually give you exactly what you expect of them. Expect a two-year-old to have a temper tantrum and that's what you'll get. Expect cooperation and positive interactions and that's what you'll get. Why not expect the best?

Tell your grandchildren how important they are to you throughout their lives.

Get to know the music your grandchildren usually listen to. You might not always like it very much, but they'll be impressed that you care enough to try.

Exercise daily and eat healthily to ensure that you are in top shape to play, travel, and engage in adventures with your grandchildren.

Have a hugging contest to determine who gives the best hugs——you or your grandchild? No matter who wins, you'll both get lots of nice hugs in the process.

Leave your stress at the door when you are with your grandchildren. Your time with them is precious, and your attention should be focused on them and not on your worries.

Practice active listening skills with your grandchildren: maintain eye contact, don't interrupt, ask questions, focus, and reflect or repeat back what was heard. Take turns, and remind them that good listening skills will make them popular with their friends.

Your teenage grandchildren may have a tough time relating to their parents. Be neutral and supportive of both of them, and if they're open to advice, suggest they be patient and listen to each other. Even if they don't see eye-to-eye, they should remember that love is always there—even through the discord.

Plan time with each of your grandchildren and let them choose an activity to do with you. If your grandchildren have siblings or loads of cousins, they may not get much one-on-one time. It will make them feel very special.

Building things together is a great way to bond with your grandchildren. A birdhouse is a great first project. Break down the work, so your grandchild gets to participate as much as you do—kids can only watch so much before they need to be actively involved.

Love letters aren't just for lovers—write little love notes to your grandchildren whenever you have a chance. Slip one in their favorite book, their pocket, on their pillow, in their book bag, under their plate, or in their suitcase, so they have a little surprise later when you're not around.

Make some hug coupons and give them to your grandchildren. Tell them they can redeem a coupon any time they need a hug. If they aren't with you, you can exchange virtual phone hugs.

Write letters to your grandchildren before they are born and throughout their lives. Even if you don't give them the letters until they are grown up, they will have a record of your love for them, as well as your thoughts about life.

When your grandchild wants to talk with you, really listen from start to finish. Parents can be too busy to listen to everything their children have to say, but you can make the time to give your grandchildren this extra special attention.

Unconditional love is priceless! No matter what your grandchildren do, make sure they know you love them.

Get out and go for a walk with your smaller grandchildren if they start acting out. Sometimes a change of scenery can be just the distraction they need to calm down.

Ask about your grandchild's day. Children often get lost in the hustle and bustle of home life and don't feel very important. They may not volunteer to share, but they sure like being asked.

Send your grandchildren notes, cards, and letters via "snail mail." In this electronic age, a letter in the post is unusual and will make your grandchild feel very special.

Give the gift of your time and attention. Giving of yourself is truly the greatest gift of all, and your grandchildren will remember you as a grandparent who cares.

Sometimes a simple hand squeeze communicates just as much love as a hug.

Grandchildren grow up so quickly and often believe they are grown up and know everything, putting on a brave face when deep inside they are still children and need some "behind the scene" help. Let them know you have confidence in them, and subtly offer them your support.

Be your grandchild's "safe place." Be the warm, loving, nurturing person they can feel comfortable with when they are hurting, sad, lonely, or tired.

Just hang out. That's right, do "nothing" with your grandchildren. No plans, no schedule—just go with the flow and be together. Those times spent hanging out may be some of the sweetest moments you have together.

It's natural for growing grandchildren to test boundaries and assert their independence. As they get older, give them opportunities to take responsibility, have their own opinions, and do things on their own. They will learn that trust is a big part of gaining their independence.

You have so many life experiences to share with your grandchildren, and it's important to emphasize the sharing aspect when talking to them about their problems. You don't have to preach to get a point across. No one likes to be lectured.

"Sticks and stones may break my bones, but words will never hurt me." A common adage, but not necessarily true. If you sense your grandchildren are being bullied at school, ask (or give them a chance to talk about it). Even if they don't have visible bruises, a bruised ego can hurt just as much, so keep your ears, eyes, and intuition open.

When your grandchildren are searching for answers as they grow up, be sure to let them know that no one has all the answers, not even you. It will take some of the pressure off them. Above all, be a good role model. Live your life in the way you would want your grandchildren to live theirs. Take good care of yourself, make healthy choices for yourself, and treat others as you'd like to be treated. They will learn more from watching you, than from anything you can ever say to them.

Do you want your grandchild to be honest and open with you? Try being "prudently" honest and open with them to encourage them to be honest with you.

Laugh at your grandchildren's jokes as if they are the funniest things you've ever heard. You should be their greatest audience.

Take the time to really get to know your grandchildren. What is really important to them? Who are their friends? What music are they listening to? What clothing styles do they like? Are they animal lovers? Do they like to cook? What sports do they like? They are precious individuals and each one is unique.

Share the lessons of your heart with your grandchildren. Tell them about a time you had your feelings hurt, what you learned, and how you came out of it OK.

As your grandchildren get older, they'll enter the exciting world of "romance"! Make sure they feel comfortable talking openly with you about their relationships, as it can be a tricky subject for them to broach with their parents. You have years of experience to share, and you'll want to know that they are safe and happy.

Pick out a special vase for each grandchild and every time you put a fresh flower in it, give your grandchild a call. You can even take a photo of the flower in their vase and email it to her.

Is your grandchild an "only" child? Perhaps when she comes to spend the night at your house she'd like to invite a friend?

Keep a journal for each grandchild with anecdotes about things they say or do. As they get older, share the stories with them. They will love to hear about themselves, and will also see how important they are to you.

Teach your grandchildren to meditate! Keep it simple: for young ones, take just a few minutes and focus on breathing together. As they get older, introduce other meditative techniques.

Bedtime rituals are a time-honored tradition. They help children chill out and settle down for sleep. Stick with whatever works best for them —a bath, a story, a massage, or music. You may also want to add some special loving touches to their bedtime routine.

Share special little rituals with your grandchild. Create a special hug or handshake, close a conversation the same way each time, or try a unique sign-off on your emails to each other. Whatever you choose, it's just between you two.

Praise your grandchildren when they behave well. This will reinforce their positive behavior, and you'll see less of their bad behavior.

It's sometimes hard to connect with older grandchildren, especially in those awkward teenage years. Their bodies and minds are changing rapidly, and mood swings can get the best of them. Even if they say something hurtful, don't let it get to you. Remind yourself that they will grow out of this phase.

Appreciation is an important skill you can teach your grandchildren. By showing them how much you appreciate your friends and family, and by telling them about the importance of lifelong friends, you will be teaching them to do the same with theirs.

Communicate with your grandkids often and treat them with respect. It's amazing how it's a two-way street, isn't it?

There is a lot of pressure on children to get good grades. Make sure that your grandchildren know it's OK if they don't get top grades, and that you have complete faith in them.

Sometimes grandparents want their grandchildren to love them so much that they are afraid to "be the boss" when they need to be. Even though you love to spoil them, remember who's the adult in the relationship and they'll respect you as well as love you.

How do you want to be remembered by your family? Are you thought of as the grandparent who is fun, silly, stern, warm, adventurous, caring, interesting, patient, grouchy, a good cook? Think about how your character may be perceived by your grandchildren and let them see your best side.

Can you hear your grandchildren? Literally. Is your hearing up to par? If not, swallow your pride and get a hearing aid. You deserve to hear some of the most important things you'll ever hear in your life.

Ask your grandchildren to tell you stories. It shows you care about what goes on in their lives and helps them to explore their creative side.

Treat your grandchildren as equals when you talk with them. Always meet them at their level and relate to them respectfully. You'll find that they actually listen to you if you do.

Encourage self-expression. Create a safe environment where your grandchildren can express themselves as individuals. Even if it means they have purple hair for a couple of months or you have to listen to them singing off-key to their favorite tune for a while, you'll find yourself reveling in their uniqueness.

When talking to your young grandchildren, move your face! Facial expressions grab their attention and make it oh so interesting for them.

Trying to get a message across to your grandchildren? Include examples they can relate to and make it real by connecting the story to their lives.

Tired of short "yes and no" conversations with your grandchildren? Try asking them open-ended questions. Instead of, "Did you have fun at school today?," ask them "What did you do in school today?".

Speak slowly and pause now and then when talking with your grandchildren or when telling them stories. Make your voice vary between soft and loud. You'll keep their attention and let them know you are focused on interacting with them.

Your grandchildren learn from your behavior. If you are comforting and loving towards them, they will treat others with the same compassion.

Be positive. At all times.

Keep cool, but don't freeze—a great motto to have and teach to your grandchildren. You will undoubtedly hit some rough spots as a grandparent, but it's important to remain calm. If your grandchildren do something you don't agree with, don't freeze them out. Stay warm and loving toward them no matter what.

Use your imagination! If you're trying to get your grandchild to be quiet while a sibling is sleeping, pretend you are in a magic forest and must not wake the sleeping princess or prince.

Surprise! Everyone loves surprises and your grandchildren are no exception. Surprise them with positive comments, phone calls, visits, presents, and snuggles.

Don't take it personally. Your grandchild's behavior may sometimes be off-kilter, but kids will be kids. It's usually to do with your grandchild coming to terms with a certain stage of his life, and is not related to anything you've done.

*Always be generous in demonstrating
your affections with hugs and snuggles
if your grandchildren like them. Your
grandchildren need lots of affection to
grow up strong, confident, and happy.
And YOU are the perfect person to
give it to them.*

When your younger grandchildren get
restless waiting for something, always
be patient and compassionate. Let
them know you understand it's hard
to wait and then distract them with a
game, joke, funny face, animal sound,
or a song.

Your grandchildren all have different personalities, and some maybe stronger or more outgoing than others. At family gatherings, make sure the quieter ones don't go unnoticed. Gently try to draw them into activities in ways that are comfortable for them, but also recognize that they may be perfectly happy playing alone from time to time.

Next time you discipline your grandchild, take a step back and ask yourself if you could have done it differently. Was it constructive or did you let your own emotions take over? You are the adult in the situation. Act like it!

Comfort your grandchildren when they cry. It's good for them to know that they are not alone in the world and that love and healing are always out there.

If you refuse to let your grandchild do or have something, tell them why. "No you may not have that candy," won't help them learn self-control. "No you may not have that candy because we are having dinner in 15 minutes," is much more effective.

If you don't see your grandchildren very often, don't be hurt if they are not comfortable or cry when they first see you. It's a good thing! It means they are learning to recognize people they know from those they don't know. Be kind and loving and they will soon warm to you.

gearing up

Are grandma and grandpa fighting over who gets to talk with the grandchildren on the phone? A good speakerphone can come in handy when no one wants to miss a word.

Grandbaby on the way? Hit the consignment shops for some great deals on the basics that will make your home baby-friendly. Ensure that any crib, high chair, stroller, or toys that you purchase aren't too out-of-date and meet current safety standards.

As a grandparent, you'll want to capture all the precious moments spent with your grandchildren. Purchase a lightweight camera that's portable. It doesn't have to be overly technical, sometimes basic cameras are better. Just make sure you have one when you need it.

Accessorize. The *Encarta Dictionary* definition of accessory is: "An optional part that may be fitted to something to perform an additional function or enhance performance." So a good thing to remember, is that it's about the love you give your grandchild and not the stuff.

Your grandchildren are stars! Be sure you're ready to capture all their best performances with an easy-to-use video camera. You'll be surprised at how small and convenient they are these days.

Keep track of your family's important events by starting an online family calendar that everyone can access from anywhere.

Get a good quality car seat for your car—your grandchildren's parents won't have to transfer their car seat back and forth when you babysit. Make sure it's installed correctly and that you know how to fasten the child into the seat.

Long-distance grandparent? You can still see your grandchildren when you talk with them. Purchase inexpensive webcams for both your computer and your children's. They are easier to use than you might think, and they will allow you to watch your grandchild grow.

Create your own family website where you and your children can post photos or videos and share stories.

Your computer is a magical place for storing photos and memorabilia of your visits with grandchildren. Online scrap booking is the latest and greatest tool. There are many websites to choose from, and you can even scan in everything from dance recital programs and train tickets to finger paint pictures and certificates.

Create a story with your grandchildren via email. You write a few lines and hit send; then they write a few lines and email it back, and so on. Before you know it, you've co-authored a story. Isn't technology a great creative tool?

Do you find yourself having lots of ideas about things your grandkids would enjoy, but then forget what they were as soon as they come to visit? A digital voice recorder can come in handy to record your ideas, or use it to record you reading a book and email them the recording.

Is your DVD player hooked up and ready to go? You'll want to keep a few fun and educational DVDs for your grandchildren— whether they are infants or young adults.

As your grandkids move into the "tween" and "teen" years, text messaging is a must! Even if texting isn't your thing, at least get proficient enough to type two sentences into your phone and send: "HRU? ILU!" (How are you? I love you!). That'll do the trick.

Whether your grandchildren live a block away or 10,000 miles away, you can play games with them in "real time" on gaming websites. Find out what computer games they like to play and get them to teach you. Be sure to check in with their parents about game choices, and make sure the sites are safe and secure.

Are your grandchildren talking about nothing but video games? To have something in common, it might be worth buying a used gaming console and a few of their favorite games. They'll be right at home when they visit your house, and you can learn to play the games enough to chat about them on the phone.

Babies come with a lot of equipment— and often the stroller, car seat, swing, and high chair are compatible—so baby can go easily from one to the other. Ask your grandchildren's parents what kind of equipment they are buying, as it might be helpful for you to have the same kind to ease transitions.

Cable, satellite, or bunny ears—your TV isn't a babysitter—but it can be a fun educational tool for your grandchildren. Make sure you check TV viewing rules with their parents.

If you can't afford loads of gadgets, equipment, and technology—don't worry. Imagination counts for a lot when it comes to entertaining grandchildren.

Take your grandchildren out to see the world. If you're into cycling tours, a bicycle trailer is the ideal vantage point for your grandchild to watch the world go by.

Music is a great tool for kids of all ages. A CD player is a must-have! And remember, you can play a CD on your computer too.

Get wired. If you don't have a personal computer—get one. If you have one but it's not up-to-date—upgrade! You'll want the latest and the greatest to organize, learn, communicate, and savor every moment of being a grandparent.

Make your home kid-friendly! Create a play corner. Put books your grandkids like to read, DVDs they like to watch, and their favorite stuffed animals on a bookcase they can reach, and get a child-size table and chairs. It will make visits a lot easier for mom and dad when they don't have to bring entertainment from their own home.

Are you a runner? Get a jogging stroller for your younger grandchildren, and they'll be happy as clams to go along for the ride.

Visit a website where you can create special books for your grandchildren. Just provide their names and they will be inserted in all the right places. Order a printed copy and voilà— your grandchildren are the lead characters in their own storybooks.

Ask your grandchild's parents for advice about products and conveniences you'd like to get for your home. Things change rapidly when it comes to children and the equipment that comes along with them.

Your garage or driveway can be an area of great interest to children. Garages are often full of tools and small easy-to-swallow objects, so it's important to keep it out of bounds. If they are playing on the driveway, make sure they are supervised.

Use your computer's Internet connection to find interesting activities to do with your grandchildren. Websites for grandparents, as well as parenting or children's websites, hold a wealth of new ideas.

Keep a supply of crayons, coloring books, and blank paper, so your grandchildren can create their own works of art. They'll come in handy when you have extra time, or if your grandchild is restless and needs something to do.

It's convenient to have a high chair at your home for visiting grandchildren. Ask their parents about the best type of age-appropriate chair, and make sure it has a seat belt and the other safety features are up-to-date. When all else fails, your lap still makes a pretty good seat for grandbaby.

A folding plastic mat you can place under baby's high chair is one of the simplest and most effective tools you'll find! Your grandchild can throw food and make a lovely mess—and all you have to do is move the chair and pick up the mat afterwards for an easy clean up!

Many babies have baths in the kitchen sink—and doesn't it make a great photo? But, there are hazards in and around the sink, so it's best to get a plastic baby bathtub designed to support baby safely.

Update your driving skills! If you are driving grandchildren around, you really do have precious cargo onboard.

Diapers are constantly being updated. You can usually trust your favorite brands, but it's best to find out which ones your grandchild's parents are using. Make sure you stock up—little ones can go through them quickly.

Babies' skin can be especially sensitive, so be sure to use shampoos and soaps that are specifically designed for little ones. They are milder, so if you do accidently get soapsuds in your grandchild's eyes it won't hurt her.

Are you ready for meals with your new grandbaby? Stock up on baby bottles (ask their mom about which kinds to get), sippy cups, child-sized silverware, and dishes. Unbreakable is the key word when it comes to feeding time.

Mobiles and mirrors, bells and chimes—all are great additions to a playpen or crib for baby. Stimulation is key, but safety is the bottom line when choosing these accessories.

You probably got along fine raising your children without a cell phone, but having one when you take your grandchildren on outings is a plus. A quick call to find out when the museum opens, the train schedule, directions to the restaurant, and of course to call in case of an emergency, can save you a lot of time and trouble. You can get a simple inexpensive phone with fewer minutes if you don't think you'll use it much.

Videophones used to be a science fiction fantasy, but not anymore! You can now get videophones that are easy to install using your home phone and your TV. What a great way to see your grandchildren more frequently.

If you have young grandchildren it's a good idea to stock up on outlet covers, safety gates, drawer locks, oven locks, fireplace screens, and bed rails. You can even get a refrigerator lock! It might seem like a lot of work, but it's better to be safe than sorry.

Before the little ones come to visit, walk slowly through each room in your home and look for safety hazards. Get down on their level, so you'll see what they might get into. You'll discover things down there you don't usually see!

Night-lights in the right places can help grandchildren feel safe at bedtime. They'll also help your grandchildren see at night if they get up to go to the bathroom. The last thing you want is for them to trip over something. Night-lights are inexpensive and can plug right into the socket—or battery-powered lights are also a great option.

Be prepared—post the poison control toll-free number near the telephone in your house, and call whenever you are concerned about something your grandchild shouldn't have eaten or touched.

If you have gas lines into your home, purchase a carbon monoxide detector to protect you and your grandchildren from poisonous gas. Test it a few times a year to ensure it's working.

Place smoke alarms throughout your house, and check the batteries at least once a year.

Don't leave your over-the-counter and prescription drugs out on the table, counter, or in a cabinet that can easily be opened by young children. Store them up high where little fingers can't reach, or in a locked cabinet. Curious kids will get into things that could be dangerous to them.

Lead paint can be deadly for young children. Get a house inspection to find out if there is any lead paint in your home, and find out whether it's best to remove it or leave it alone. Check your baby furniture and toys too—especially older items.

If you have a swimming pool, it's best that this is fenced off with a gate that you can lock. Young grandchildren can easily fall into open pools or ponds, so it's wise to keep these off-limits unless an adult supervises them. It only takes a moment for a young child to drown.

Soothing music and natural sound CD's are great to have on hand for nap time or if grandchildren are sleeping over at your house. You'll find a great selection for babies and children, from classical music to animal sounds or rain and waterfalls. Be careful, you may fall asleep too.

Safety is an ongoing process. Regularly check all baby equipment, toys, furniture, outdoor swings, and slides—anything your grandchildren come in contact with—to ensure there are no safety risks.

Do you have stairs in your home? If you have young grandchildren, be sure you block the staircase with a safety gate. Little ones move quickly, and stairs are the most likely place for them to take a tumble.

Do your grandchildren have allergies? Find out from their parents any sensitivities they may have—animals, food, grasses, trees, dust, cleaning fluids, strong scents, or even fabrics can all be allergens and you'll want to be prepared.

Turn down the temperature gauge on your hot water tank, so your grandchildren will not get burnt accidentally.

If you visit a local playground
with your grandchildren, take a
look and make sure it is safe.
You can call the local authority
and ask about how frequently the
playground has safety inspections.

*If you have little ones coming to
your home, make sure you put
cleaning supplies out of reach. Even
everyday household cleaning fluids,
powders, and soaps can be
dangerous to them.*

Make your bathroom kid-friendly.
Non-skid bath mats in the tub will
help to prevent your grandchildren
from slipping…and you too.

Ask the local fire department to come to your house and give you safety tips. If your grandchildren sleep or play on the second or third level, is there a safe way for them to get out in the event of a fire?

Get a small stool with non-skid rubber on the bottom for your grandchildren to stand on when washing their hands at the sink. It will help keep them safe, and a handrail is an added plus.

The knickknacks you've gathered over the years may be very tempting for little hands. Glass and ceramic objects can be very dangerous, especially if they break. When your grandchildren come to visit, move these out of reach.

Examine your furniture for sharp edges, loose pieces, or latches; chairs with weak seats or backs; and anything else that could be hazardous to children. These things may be easy for you to steer clear of, but your grandchildren don't have the same abilities you have.

Your grandchildren can get into the darndest places in a split second. Think small, and make sure there are no hidden spots in your house or yard where they might get stuck.

Trash bags, packing boxes, grocery bags, bits of rope, and dog leashes can all be hazardous to young children. Organize your house so they are hidden away, or make sure your grandchildren are supervised if they are within reach.

When it comes to the safety of your grandchildren, the most important thing is supervision, supervision, and supervision.

"Fragile—handle with care" means just that! If you have glass objects, particularly tables, in your home, teach young grandchildren to be very careful with them or move them out of bounds. It seems like kids are drawn to the very things that can hurt them the most.

Once you throw something in the trash, it may be out of your mind, but it may be within your grandchild's reach! Empty your wastebaskets before a visit from your younger grandchildren, then cover or place them up high where they can't be reached.

Are your grandchildren crawling? The floor can hold dangers for infants and toddlers that adults don't even notice. Wipe up spills right away, move pet food and kitty litter to a safe place, and keep an eye out for sharp objects, such as nails or tiny staples, that could hurt your grandbaby.

Bath time is fun time, but when it's over make sure you drain the water from the tub immediately. Children can die in just a few inches of water.

It's fun for grandchildren to help with laundry chores. They are often fascinated by the machines, clothes, detergents, and spray stain removers. It can be a great activity to do together, but make sure your utility area is off limits to little ones when you're not around. Dryers can get very hot, and little ones could suffocate if they crawled inside. Detergents may also be mistaken for colorful drinks, so stay with them at all times if you do decide to let them help you with the washing.

Childproofing latches on kitchen, bathroom, and medicine cabinets will allow you to relax and enjoy your grandchildren when they visit, without worrying about them getting into danger.

If you're a hot coffee or tea drinker, keep the pot—and your cup—far out of reach for young grandchildren.

Microwave popcorn is a great treat. It's fun to watch the bag expand when it pops, and it's good to eat while watching TV or a movie together. To prevent burns, make sure the steam is directed away from you and your grandchildren when you open the bag, and let the hot kernels cool down before eating.

Teach your grandchildren about safety and what can happen if they don't follow safety rules. You don't want to scare them too much, but giving them a real idea of consequences will help them understand. Science websites are great for explaining how hot water can burn or why oil catches fire.

Matches are of great interest to young children, so be sure to lock them up along with lighters and anything else that can cause fire.

Have a fire drill! Help your grandchildren practice what they would do if there were a fire in your home, including making them aware of safe exits. Remember the old reliable "stop, drop, and roll" if their clothing should ever catch fire.

Cooking is a favorite activity for grandparents and grandchildren. If you use the stove, place pots on back burners with the handles facing away, so children's little hands can't reach them.

You want your grandchildren to have fun at your house, and often games like tag or hide-and-seek are big hits. Just make sure there are no loose throw rugs on the floor they could slip on as they rush through the house.

If you have sliding glass doors or storm doors with glass, place removable stickers on them so grandchildren don't crash through them when they run in and out of the house.

Isn't sliding down the banister fun? Yes, but someone could end up with a sore tushy if they fall off the end. If you allow your grandkids to banister-slide, be sure you supervise so you can catch them if they start to fall.

You may have baby equipment left over from your older grandchildren, but even if it's only a few years old, make sure it meets current safety standards. Don't take any risks with your grandchild's safety.

Read children's books about safety issues to your little ones. Sometimes the message is clearer when they hear about a favorite storybook character who learns about not touching hot things or throwing balls inside the house.

Talk with your grandchildren about safety rules in your house. Post your rules on a bulletin board where they are easy to see, and review the rules from time to time. Even before they can read, they'll get the picture.

If your home is difficult to "kid-proof,"
create a special safe corner or room where
grandchildren spend most of their time.
They'll feel more comfortable knowing their
boundaries, and you'll be able to relax more.

We all have so many electronics
these days—and multiple outlets
can be dangerous for little children
who like to stick things in them.
Look for a "shock-proof" surge
protector that prevents children
from inserting foreign objects.

Don't assume that toys are safe just because
they are new. Check consumer product safety
websites and use common sense when you get
toys for grandchildren. Look the toy over for
sharp edges, lead paint, small pieces that
could be swallowed, and other hazards.

Help your grandchildren learn to clean up after themselves to prevent tripping over toys left on the floor, pets eating leftover food, or fire hazards.

Cars are fun for grandchildren to explore, but make sure you supervise them and always engage the emergency break. The last thing you want is your grandchild rolling the car down the driveway into oncoming traffic.

A pint-sized chair, which is a perfect fit for your grandchild, will make her feel right at home. You can find rocking chairs just for kids, or even nicely stuffed armchairs just their size.

Pets are important members of many families. Take the time to carefully familiarize your grandchildren with your pets, and teach them both how to interact safely and lovingly with each other.

Your grandchildren may love your pets—and may think of them as toys. Know your pets' limits, and be sure your little ones know that pets aren't to be dressed, ridden, put in boxes, or taken for rides in strollers.

Kids are kids, and no matter how much you safety-proof your home, accidents will still happen. Be prepared, as best you can be, and then relax and allow kids to do the same. It's not fun for them if they are afraid to touch anything or to move freely in your home.

Where are your first aid supplies? Can you get to them easily? It's a good idea to have an up-to-date first aid kit with antiseptic, antibiotic ointment, bandages, and other supplies. Place it where young grandchildren can't reach it, but where you can get to it quickly and easily.

Keep a list of important phone numbers near your phone, particularly contact details for your grandchild's doctor and parents. It's also a good idea to include important information about your grandchild by your phone, such as their age, weight, any medications they take, and any allergies they may have. You may need this information in an emergency or if anything happens to you, so that a friend or neighbor can access it quickly.

When you take your grandchildren for a ride in your car, you are taking their lives in your hands. Educate yourself about the child safety seat laws in your area or in the areas to which you may travel. Remember that the laws and guidelines change as a child grows.

One of the most important things you can do to improve your grandchild's safety in the car is to be a good role model. Wear your seatbelt at all times—children learn from what you do.

Consult your car owner's manual to find out if you should disengage the airbags when your grandchild is riding in your car.

It is generally safest for children to ride in the back seat of the car. They may not like it, but doesn't safety come first?

Never, ever leave your grandchild alone in the car—not even for a few minutes. Children often get trapped in cars or accidentally put the car into gear; but worst of all, your car could get stolen with your grandchild in it.

When grandchildren are around, check behind the car before you back out of the driveway. A bicycle might be in the way, but more importantly a small child could be there. Unfortunately, it happens all the time. Check and double check. Always.

Place your car keys out of reach, including your car's remote entry devices. They seem like fun toys, and grandchildren may be tempted to use them and could become trapped in the car trunk.

Never let your young grandchildren get out of the car by themselves, especially if you park on the street or in a crowded parking lot. It only takes a split second for them to dash out in front of a car.

Keep hot foods away from the edge of the counter or table when you have little ones underfoot. Family gatherings often get hectic, and it only takes one false move to knock that dish over and burn whoever is standing below.

Grandpa and grandma only have two hands! Don't try to do too many things at once while holding your grandchild. It's tempting to have a grandchild on one hip and be pouring coffee with the other hand. Don't do it—no cup of coffee is worth the risk.

Children are fascinated with gadgets in the kitchen. Supervise the use of blenders, microwaves, can openers, food processors, and other kitchen tools or machines, so no one gets carried away.

As part of your safety plan when your grandchildren are visiting, choose a family meeting place outside the home where you will all meet in case of a fire or other emergency.

Are you a gardener? Plants can bring wonderful life and energy to a home. If you have tiny grandchildren around be sure they aren't tempted to nibble on toxic leaves, roots, or bulbs.

Be prepared with lots of high protection sunscreen when you take the grandchildren to ANY outdoor summer activity—not just when going to the beach.

The bathtub faucet can dole out some nasty bumps and bruises. Try an inflatable faucet cover or a fun plastic animal head cover to entertain your grandchildren. They are available at most baby stores and are easy to install—most just slip over the faucet.

Worried about growing babies and toddlers being able to reach up and open a closed door? You can place a plastic doorknob cover and lock on almost any kind of door handle, which makes it impossible for little hands to open.

Many homes have mini-blinds in the windows——be sure to tie up the hanging cords so little ones don't get tangled up in them.

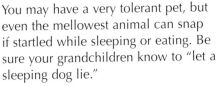

You may have a very tolerant pet, but even the mellowest animal can snap if startled while sleeping or eating. Be sure your grandchildren know to "let a sleeping dog lie."

Race for it! If you want your grandchild to do something, turn it into a race to see who gets it done first. Your grandchild will usually want to win!

Get some paints and decorate a flowerpot with your grandchildren, then plant some seeds or a small plant. It will make a nice gift for mom.

Get on their level. That's right—get on the floor, sit in the kiddy chairs, or sit your grandchildren up on a table. You'll communicate better eye-to-eye at any age—even if they aren't yet talking.

Summertime is a great season to be out in the backyard. Buy some outdoor games, like croquet or lawn tennis, or a splashing pool and a beach ball to toss around. Get your grandchildren away from the television or computer games and out in the sunshine. They have all winter to be inside.

Have a budding artist in the family? Get your grandchildren a large poster-board and have them create a poster of your entire family. Include everyone—even the family pets! Have it the poster laminated and you'll have a keepsake for years to come.

Plant a garden with your grandchildren. Water and weed together. As your garden grows, so will your relationship.

What was your favorite game as a child? Play it with your grandchildren. Vintage games are easy to find on websites, and many of the games you played while growing up are still popular. You'll have fun and your grandchildren will learn more about you.

Have an old-fashioned Ice Cream Social. Get creative about the toppings, including traditional hot fudge sauce as well as unusual things, like cereal, jam, or brightly colored candy. Let your grandkids make their own sundae and watch them get creative with their toppings. Don't worry if they can't eat it all, just enjoy the experience of making something together.

Make up secret, silly nicknames for each other. Peanut, huggy bear, pickle nose, nano, top pop, gabby—whatever the two of you can agree upon. The sillier the better.

Gather some wood, a hammer and nails, and glue, and build a tree house for your grandchildren. Better yet, build it together. Make it your grandchildren's special place in your yard.

Make storytelling a trip in your imagination—the more outlandish the better! A recurring character, who perhaps has your grandchild's name spelt backwards or shares their characteristics, is a special touch that will definitely spark their interest.

Tea for two—or three, or four—is a fun way to use those beautiful teacups you have in your cupboard. Dress up, wear hats and necklaces, eat finger sandwiches and cookies, and pretend to be proper adults at a tea party. Your grandchildren will love it. A little weak tea with a spot of sugar goes a long way.

Plan a family talent show—or better yet—a "no talent" show! See who can put on the worst act and offer a fun prize for the winner.

Teach your grandchildren about one of your hobbies. You may collect coins, watch movies, ski, cycle, fix cars, sew, or garden. Whatever it is, bring it to their level and give them a glimpse of the things you really enjoy doing. You may end up with a hobby in common.

Grab a dictionary and choose a word that no one recognizes. One grandchild writes down the dictionary definition and all the others make up definitions. The child who wrote the real definition reads all the made-up definitions along with the actual definition. Everyone else has to guess which one is the REAL one. It's a fun game for all ages.

A swing set in your own backyard will make it a fun play area for your grandchildren.

Do your young grandchildren get ants in their pants while they have to wait for a table at a restaurant, a doctor's appointment, or a long plane ride? Try finger puppets. They are small and easy to carry in your purse or pocket, and both grandchild and you can wear them and tell each other stories to stay occupied.

Be spontaneous! Sometimes the best memories are created out of unplanned moments of adventure and joy.

Have a contest among your grandchildren and offer a prize! Who can read the most books, hold their breath the longest, set the table fastest, eat the most pancakes, collect the most for charity, finish a mile walk, get dressed the fastest? Offer a prize to the winner—and make sure your contests offer opportunities to win for all your grandchildren.

What game can you play without a board or props? Hide and go seek! Any home has many hiding places for young children, and don't forget to pretend you can't see them.

Everyone loves the movies! Co-produce a home video with your grandchild. The finished product will be something you can watch over and over again.

Get out the construction paper, scissors, glue, and markers, and make greeting cards with your grandchildren. They can decorate and sign their cards, and you can help them give the cards to family members when birthdays or holidays come up.

Have a joke contest via email with your grandchild—see who can keep coming back with jokes. A little shared laughter can go a long way.

Don't be afraid to cheer on your favorite sports team with your grandchildren. They'll get excited with you, and you'll develop a bond around watching games and matches together. Get them a t-shirt or hat that matches yours and they'll be your biggest fans.

Help your grandchild write a play and perform it for the family.

Learn a new skill with your grandchild. Starting out at the same level allows you to learn together, instead of one of you being the teacher. It will be a great shared experience you'll never forget. Learn piano, calligraphy, dance, golf, or painting—whatever interests you both.

Yoga for kids is all the rage and might be right at your level, too! Go to a class or watch a kids' yoga DVD with your grandchild, so you can stretch and get flexible together. If it's tough for you to get down on the floor, adapt the poses and do them from your chair.

Get a little wet! Take out your galoshes, umbrella, and slicker, and take a walk in the rain with your grandchildren. The outdoors is transformed when it rains, and splashing in and out of puddles can be loads of fun!

Have fun with your grandchild while also getting into shape. Jumping rope together will help your grandchild burn off excess energy and help you burn off calories.

*Be a monster, but in a good way!
Playing scary monster games is a great
way for your grandchild to learn that
we all have things we fear, and that's
OK. Remind them that behind the
monster face it's really just harmless
grandma or grandpa.*

Got water? Got balloons? Why not
have water balloon fights with your
grandchildren? They'll love getting
soaked without getting into trouble,
and even more, they'll enjoy
getting you wet.

An impromptu piggyback ride for a small
grandchild is a special treat. Make sure
you stay in shape and protect your back,
so you're capable of giving the odd
piggyback here and there.

Plant a rose bush in your yard for each grandchild. Choose their favorite color and name it for them. You can give them updates on their rose when you talk on the phone, and when they visit they will be able water and pick the roses themselves. A sachet of petals or a dried rose from their bush might make a nice memento too.

Animals are a big favorite with children. A visit to the zoo can keep children entertained for hours, or even a walk with your dog, a visit with the neighbors' cats, or bird watching can bring amusement.

There is an old expression, "Music soothes the savage beast." Even if your grandchildren aren't considered beasts, they may need soothing from time to time. Keep a collection of soothing classical or children's music on hand.

Do you remember your favorite games as a child? Your favorite toys? There are many original vintage games and toys available now, or newly made imitations. Get your favorites and introduce them to your grandchildren. Some things are just classics, and you'll enjoy the memories they bring back of your own childhood.

What are your grandchildren's hopes and dreams? Work together to create a collage of magazine pictures that illustrate the things your grandkids want to achieve during their lifetime.

Sing like no one is listening! Teach your grandchildren your favorite songs, and don't worry about how well you sing. Music is for everyone—experience the joy of making it with your grandchildren.

What's the most portable game when you're on the go with grandchildren? A deck of cards. Pull out a deck and presto you have entertainment.

If you have granddaughters, have a home spa day. After checking with mom and dad, paint those little finger and toenails, style hair, and have a blast.

Dance, dance, dance! Get moving with your grandchildren to the music they like, then try the music you like—everybody gets a turn. Leave your self-consciousness at the door, and your grandchildren will get a big kick out of grandparents who groove.

Make up a simple song to a familiar tune with your grandchild's name and their favorite toy. "Curious George and Elizabeth, riding in the car…" to the tune of Old MacDonald may be a big family hit.

Have a tickling contest. Who can go the longest without laughing? Remember, it's all in fun, so know when enough is enough.

If you have grandbabies, you might want to purchase a baby monitor intercom. They also come in handy as children get older, especially if you want to keep an ear open to make sure they are playing safely in another room.

Taking your grandchildren for their first grown-up haircut at the beauty salon can be a fun tradition. Check with mom and dad first, and make sure your grandchildren want to get their haircut. Make an occasion of it —have lunch out afterwards!

Do you have a group of grandchildren coming to your house? Set up stations around your home with different games and toys. Blow a whistle every five minutes and tell them to rotate to the next station. You'll keep them occupied and channel all their excess energy.

Teach your grandchild how to make a bouquet of flowers. Pick them from your yard, or go to the flower store together and pick out your favorites. Take the time to cut, arrange, and display the bouquet and take a picture of your handy work.

Soap it up! Collect small pieces of leftover soap, put them in a blender along with a little scented oil or some dried herbs, and add a little water. Blend well. Put the mixture in an ovenproof glass dish and heat gently. Pour the mixture into a mold and let it solidify. Voilà! You and your grandchild are soap-makers.

Walk it out! When young children can't sit still or focus on an activity for long, you can always just take a walk. Go for a stroll around the house, around the yard, or up the street. You'll be amazed how the smallest things, like bugs on the sidewalk, will keep them entertained.

Stairs can be very entertaining for toddlers. Up and down...and up and down...and...you get the picture. Yes, it's repetitive and you may get a little bored, but it will keep them busy for quite a while. Just make sure you are there to keep them safe.

Create a lantern out of a gourd or pumpkin for some old-fashioned fun. Who needs to wait for Halloween to make a jack-o-lantern? Carve out flowers or other designs and insert a candle.

Children are full of curiosity, and there are plenty of opportunities for exploration right in your own home. A grand adventure can be had in the exciting horticultural world of your backyard. Explore things together. What makes things grow? How do machines work? Even something as simple as how do doors open and close?

Television can be a great learning tool when it is used in conjunction with real-life activities. For example, try watching a gardening show with your grandchildren, then put what you've learned into action by working on your garden together.

Your grandsons might not be interested in a spa day like your granddaughters, but they'll love temporary tattoos!

Gardening can be a year-round pastime no matter where you live. In the winter, get out the gardening books and enlist your grandchildren to help plan your spring planting. Draw the design and research the plants and flowers—a little winter garden dreaming can provide a big lift.

Teach your grandchild how to make their own tea using herbs from your garden. Lemon balm makes a great sweet tea. It's easy—just gather herbs together, hang them to dry, then use the dried herbs in your tea strainer.

Make simple homemade finger paints with two cups of flour, two cups of cold water, and food coloring. Get out the paper and let the kids have fun! Be prepared for brightly colored little fingers, but it will wash off, eventually.

Do you get frustrated with the wasted paper that you end up with when you print emails or website articles? Don't waste them—turn them over and give them to your grandchildren for their drawings and paintings. Children can be prolific artists and you'll end up putting that paper to good use. Recycle any artwork they don't want to keep.

Bird-watch in your own backyard! Give your grandchildren their very own set of binoculars and a children's bird book, and keep a notebook handy to record each time you see a different species of bird.

Your grandkids will love gardening with you if they have their own gardening tools that are just the right size. Get them a rake, shovel, spade, and gloves. Teach them how to use, clean, and care for their tools.

Are your grandchildren your gardening buddies? Make them their own gardening apron or jacket, with plenty of pockets and places to hang their gardening tools.

Have fun with daily tasks, such as cleaning, cooking, or doing laundry, with your grandchildren. Turn it into a game and get them to take pride in their daily chores. You can be a great role model and teach them life skills at the same time.

Take a "scent walk" through your herb or flower garden.
Blindfold your grandchildren and hold their hands as you
walk through the herbs—or hold a piece up for them to
smell. See if they can identify the various herbs or flowers
by smell alone.

Put up your "Gone Fishing" sign, grab the fishing poles, and take your grandchildren to the nearest river, pond, lake, or ocean. Oversee the baiting of the hook carefully, and be sure to brief the kids on fishing safety. Let them know that half the fun of fishing is just being there—in case they don't catch anything!

Practice insect "catch and release" with your grandkids by helping them collect bugs, caterpillars, worms, and other creepy crawlies in a glass jar. Take photos, look up the insects on the Internet, and help them make their own bug book. When you've finished, release the critters back to nature.

Go with the flow! You may have a fun activity planned, but if it's not clicking with your grandkids don't force it. Be spontaneous. Your grandchildren will love you more for your flexibility.

Take your grandchild with you to volunteer at the local animal shelter. They'll learn about giving back and have fun with the pups at the same time.

Take your grandchildren to yard, garage, rummage, or jumble sales. Give them a small allowance to spend, and have fun looking at all the treasures as well as the junk.

Switch roles with your grandchild. Let the younger one be in charge, while you pretend to be the grandchild. You can even make masks of each other and wear them along with articles of each other's clothing.

Play the color game. Pick a color and have your grandchild point out things of that color all day long—everywhere you go! When they reach 100 there should be a prize—of that color of course.

Your dining room table can be transformed into a tent, a fairyland, a cave, or a cabin by simply hanging blankets off the sides. Help your grandkids create their own fantasyland in your own dining room.

If mom and dad approve, take your grandchildren for swimming lessons. It might be a fun extra their parent's can't quite handle, and it will give them good exercise and a potentially lifesaving skill.

food and festivities

Got the grandchildren for a week? Sit down with them and plan menus with their favorite foods. Assign tasks to each grandchild, so they can each play an active role and help with cooking, setting tables, and cleaning up. Make sure you post your menus at kid height.

Have a silly supper with your grandchildren with a menu of whatever is in your cupboard, even if it absolutely does not go together or seem like a meal. Macaroni and cheese and pickles, leftover pizza and ice cream, hot dogs, pancakes and black olives. Be creative—the sillier the better.

Next time you make a cake, wrap some coins in foil and put them in the cake mixture before you bake. Your grandchildren will have a good time finding the coins as they eat, but make sure they know the coins are there, so no teeth are damaged.

Once in a while, have dessert as a first course. Your grandchildren will love the surprise.

Fix healthy snacks for your grandkids. Fruit, nuts, and veggies will help them grow up strong, healthy, and ready to learn. You are their role model. Show them that you eat healthily, too.

Do you have a tradition of making certain favorite family recipes? Take time to teach your grandchildren how to make them. Don't worry if they don't get it the first time. Make it an annual ritual, and as they grow older they'll take pride in knowing how to make the time-tested traditional recipes everyone loves.

Go for a picnic! Picnics are inexpensive and enough of an event to make a fuss over. Whether you picnic on the living room floor, your own backyard, or a beautiful park, it's a change of scenery and makes even everyday food taste special.

When you take your grandchildren on an outing, let them pack their own lunches. Have healthy choices available for them to choose from, but let them have the final say on which ones go into their sack lunch. Put them in charge of carrying their own lunch. This is a great way to teach good nutrition and responsibility at the same time.

When was the last time you squeezed lemons to make your own lemonade? Try it with your grandchildren—it's a sticky, sweet delight that they'll enjoy because they helped make it.

Create a family recipe book. Write out your own family favorites, and collect more from your children, extended family, and even your grandchildren, who may have a few things they'd like to contribute! It will be an heirloom that generations to come can use and feel connected to.

A good way to cook with your grandchildren is to break down recipes into specific tasks. List the tasks and keep a note of the steps you will have to do for safety reasons. Go over the plan with them briefly before you start, and be prepared to skip steps, or do some of theirs if their short attention spans get the better of them.

Your youngest grandchildren can help you wash vegetables under cold water. Let them know what an important job they have, and then find something else for them to do while you cut the veggies.

Setting the table can be a fun activity—not just a chore! Allow your grandchildren to experiment with different tablecloths and napkins, dishes, and table décor. Who cares if the knife and fork aren't in the right spots—they are creating a work of art.

Before a young grandchild is ready to use a knife, they can use a cheese grater. It's good practice to start with something that has some sharp edges, but is safer to use than a knife. Make macaroni and cheese and let your grandchild grate the cheese, so they feel included.

Make a salad together and discuss the different parts of vegetables that are used—stems, leaves, roots, fruit, and flowers. Your grandchildren will learn a lot and have a yummy nutritious meal at the same time.

Stir things up! Stirring is a favorite pastime of young children. Almost any dish you make has some opportunity for a grandchild to be involved with stirring.

Does your grandchild measure up? Literally, that is. Give your grandchild the job of measuring out ingredients with cups and spoons for your favorite recipe. It's a great way for them to start learning about cooking.

Making cutout cookies is a popular grandparent and grandchild activity. However, it can be a long, multi-stepped endeavor, and you often lose their attention along the way. Try making the dough ahead of time, then have your grandchild help roll and cut the cookies. Make the icing together. It takes less time and still involves plenty of measuring and stirring, and your grandchild can get creative with colors.

As your grandchildren get older, they will enjoy using the gadgets in your kitchen. Opening cans, running the blender, holding the mixer—and you know who gets to lick the beaters.

Plant a vegetable garden with your grandchild. Nurture it together and then cook with the fruits of your labor. There is a greater sense of satisfaction when you cook with food that you've grown. Your grandchild will also learn a lot about tending to plants.

Make bread with your grandchildren. Kneading dough by hand is a great way to burn off excess energy, and when the dough rises it's like a miracle—no matter what your age.

Make family history come to life by teaching your grandchildren how to make their favorite family recipes. Look at photos of the family member from whom the recipe came, and share stories and your memories of them with your grandchild.

Give your grandchild their very own children's cookbook. Make it a tradition to cook a recipe from their cookbook every time he visits. Take photos and celebrate the results, even if it doesn't turn out exactly perfect.

Use cooking as a practical way to teach math. Measuring ingredients uses basic math, and better yet, doubling a recipe or cutting it in half uses calculation skills.

Looking for some good, wholesome television for grandchildren? Many children love watching cooking shows. They are entertained and learn something at the same time. Watch your favorite show, then try out the recipes together for a well-rounded experience.

Get organized and let your grandkids help. The kitchen is a great place for kids to learn organization and planning skills by making grocery lists, organizing dishes in the cupboards, or taking an inventory of canned goods.

Do you have recipes on bits of paper scattered all around your house? Enlist your grandchildren to help you gather all your recipes and categorize them, then use the computer to create your own personal recipe collection. You'll have a family keepsake—and your grandchildren will be a part of it.

Every cook needs an apron!
Get a plain white child-sized
chef apron and decorate it
yourself with your grandchild's
name. Little girls will love
some "bling" on their aprons.

A trip to the grocery store can be a grand
adventure. Take you grandchild and take
your time. Look at all the unusual foods.
Things you take for granted will be
fascinating to younger children. And
many grocery stores have mini-grocery
carts for children to push. It just doesn't
get any better than that, does it?

Get on the Internet with your grandchild and research some of the odder things that people eat. Cactus, buffalo, snake, eel, flowers, and of course, chocolate covered ants are a big favorite!

If your grandchildren are helping you in the kitchen, they'll love having their very own child-sized hot pads and mitts, spoons, whisks, and other cooking utensils. Most cooking stores will have just what you'll need.

A safe, stable stool that will bring your little ones up to table level is a must if you have grandchildren who like to cook.

Baking a cake, pie, cookies, or bread? Get your grandchildren involved with mini loaf pans, cupcakes, mini pie tins, and small cookie sheets. Not only will they love the pans—they'll love having baked goods just their size to eat.

Make mealtime, family time. Set rules for everyone (including you) about TV, phones, and video games during meals, and put the emphasis on talking and enjoying each other. It may be the only time you can get your grandchildren to sit still.

Research shows that memories are stimulated by our sense of smell. The scent of baking bread, hot apple cider, cookies in the oven, and other favorites, will forever bring back your grandchildren's pleasant memories of time spent with you.

Soothing music during meals is a great way to calm your grandchildren down and create a pleasant atmosphere for eating and conversation.

Got "cabin fever" during the winter? Bring some green into your home by planting a herb garden with your grandchildren. One pot, placed in a sunny spot, can hold several herbs. The more you cut herbs the more they grow, so use them when you cook to show your grandchildren the connection between gardening and cooking.

*Have a nosey contest with your grandchildren.
No, not who has the biggest nose, but the most
accurate one. Blindfold your grandchildren and set
out several small dishes with spices from your
cabinet. Have them smell and guess what the spice
is. Cinnamon is a big favorite!*

An important part of cooking is the clean up. Get a child-sized broom and a dustpan, so your grandchild can participate.

Make herbed vinegars and oils with your grandchildren. They can help cut and wash the herbs, measure the liquids, and place the herbs in the jars. They can even draw labels and stick them on the jars. Homemade vinegars and oils make great presents for friends and family.

Making jams and jellies is becoming a lost art. Why not make some with your grandchildren? Savor all the steps together: preparing the jars, picking and washing the berries, extracting the juice, filling the jars, and of course, eating the results.

Water, water everywhere— and LOTS of drops for you! Encourage your grandkids to drink water, and be a good role model by drinking lots yourself. Water will help you stay healthy and will help your grandchild's growing body as well. Save the soda pop for special occasions.

Don't wait for a hot summer day to make homemade ice cream—it's popular any day! There are some good shortcut recipes using pudding mix, and you can get an electric ice-cream maker if you want to save your arms from all that churning! Your grandchildren will love it, especially if you make their favorite flavors.

Make popsicles more fun by getting your grandchildren to make their own! Just make juice, lemonade, or another favorite beverage, and pour it into ice-cube trays or popsicle molds. A great thirst quencher on a hot summer day.

Oh nuts! Cracking them, that is. Your grandchildren will love to help use the nutcracker to crack nuts. They may not like to eat them as they are, but you could try putting them in some yummy cookies?

Have a "sleep-tight-nighty-night" holiday pajama tradition. Give your grandchildren special festive pajamas for each holiday. They'll anticipate them each holiday season, and they won't want that tradition to end even after they are out of footy pajamas.

Before you head to the grocer with your grandchild, have them help you cut out coupons. Be sure you have safe, age-appropriate scissors.

Religious holidays can hold potential for family tensions, particularly if family members have varying religious views. If there is a holiday that is meaningful to you, take the lead on planning a get-together. Learn about the other religions in your family and respect their practices. Many families do well by blending religious traditions for shared value and meaning.

Help your grandchildren learn that holidays aren't just about getting expensive gifts. Teach them the joy of giving by helping them make a list of family and friends for their gift list. If you have some craft supplies, make homemade gifts from them, or take the kids shopping for carefully chosen inexpensive ones to give.

Create a special ornament for the holidays with a photo of you and your grandchild —it will trigger many happy memories in your grandchild's future.

Be the holiday grandparent! Plan something special for your grandchildren for every holiday you can think of— from St. Valentine's Day to Arbor Day or Christmas, Kwanzaa, Hanukkah, the first day of Summer, Friendship Day, and don't forget April Fool's day for some funny jokes.

Children love parties—big and small. Holidays are a great excuse for a party! Pull out the noisemakers, decorations, candles, and cake, and you've got a celebration.

Celebrate holidays, but on the wrong dates. Have a Christmas celebration in July, or Halloween in April. Your grandkids will love the silliness of it, and will enjoy the activities just as much as they do on the proper dates.

Create your grandchild's own calendar, including events like their first day of big school, the date they scored their first football goal, or even their first date. Update the calendar every year, and celebrate the big and the little triumphs in their lives.

If you celebrate Christmas, help your grandchildren track Santa's progress to your house on Christmas Eve by visiting www.noradsanta.org. You can watch Santa's progress in six languages.

Create a place in your home where grandchildren will always know you'll have a special holiday decoration or two. The holiday corner will become one of their favorite places to go when they come to your house.

Have you ever missed a family birthday? Devastating, isn't it? As your family grows, it gets harder to keep track of all the birthdays, anniversaries, graduations, and other important dates. Get a perpetual birthday calendar that has the dates of every month without a year. Hang it in a place you'll see easily every day (some people hang them in their bathrooms), so you'll know ahead of time what special occasions to plan for each month.

Start a "first day of school" tradition with your grandchildren, but make sure it doesn't conflict with anything planned by their parents. Make a special snack for their lunch, write a note for them to carry or read that morning, take photos, or call them after school to hear all about it.

There are always beloved recipes associated with the holidays. Create a holiday recipe book with a collection of those family favorites. Your grandmother's plum pudding or mother's potato latkes recipes should be easy to find when the holidays arrive. You'll use it for years to come, and so will your grandchildren.

Put some hot chocolate in a thermos and walk around your neighborhood with your grandkids for a holiday lights tour. If it's too far to walk, jump in the car. Delight in the simple pleasure of those lights reaching out from a stranger's home or garden to say "happy holidays!"

Make fruit exciting—make a fruit salad! It may be hard to get your grandchildren to eat fruit, but if you involve them in the cutting and mixing for the fruit salad, they'll get more excited about it— and they may even dare to try a bit.

Unfortunately, holidays can be both joyous and stressful. Sometimes the scales get tipped toward the stressful side when the family goes into overdrive. Try to prevent your grandkids from feeling the pressure by letting go a little. It doesn't have to be perfect for them. Their fondest memories will be of the most basic family traditions.

As your family grows, it may be necessary to change traditions and holiday celebrations to accommodate grandchildren's schedules, multiple family members, varying locations, and also your co-grandparents. Deal with it. Adapt and go with the flow. Just do your best to ensure your grandchildren remember the holidays as a time of family togetherness and fun.

While traditions are important, they sometimes become outdated. Don't hang on to those that aren't working. Cherish the memories of them, and create new traditions that fit in with the different interests and ages of your grandchildren.

At the end of each year, make a holiday photo album with an entire year's worth of photos and memorabilia. It will be fun for the grandchildren to look at them over the years and laugh at that outdated hairstyle or wild outfit grandma was wearing, or remember much-loved presents.

If you celebrate Christmas, have a separate "grandchildren's tree" and showcase any of their homemade ornaments.

The holidays offer a great excuse to celebrate family traditions. Grandchildren love knowing that the same things will happen every year, even if there are slight changes from time to time.

If your children do not practice your religion, ask them if they would mind if you share it with your grandchildren and to what extent. If they say "no," you will have to accept it. Under no circumstances should you "sneak" your religion into your grandchildren's lives.

If your children are divorced or you are a step-grandparent, accept the fact that you may not have an entire holiday with your grandkids. Many families split up the days. Try to carve out a few special hours and be happy with them.

learn and grow

Go green—teach your grandchildren about recycling. You'll want the earth to share it's bounties in the future, so your grandchildren and great-grandchildren can also enjoy them.

Read to your grandchildren from the time they are tiny. Picture books, storybooks, magazines, and novels—all will help your grandchild learn and love to read. Just make sure the subject matter is OK with mom and dad.

Start a book club with your grandchildren. Read the same books and then talk about them on the phone, via email, on a website, or over dinner. You might be surprised at how much you enjoy reading the books they like, and you'll have some really good conversations.

Getting your grandchildren to brush their teeth isn't always easy. Buy them a special toothbrush, which features their favorite cartoon character, and a yummy flavored toothpaste to use at your house. Soon they will be on their way to a healthy, brilliant smile.

Listen to your grandchildren read—be their best audience. Not only will you enjoy it, your patience and attention will help them learn.

Volunteer with your grandchildren. There are many service opportunities in your community—contact your local volunteer office or charity to find out how you can give together. Your grandchildren will learn the ethic of volunteerism and service through action.

Most kids have a natural curiosity, and science experiments can be fun and educational. Visit a science website with ideas for simple activities for kids, using supplies you already have in your home.

Teach your grandchildren about classical music by listening to pieces and making up stories about what the music is telling you. Sergei Prokofiev's "Peter and the Wolf" is a great one to start with.

Teach your grandchildren about conservation by starting a compost pile in your yard. When they visit, have them collect eggshells, coffee grounds, leaves, and other goodies for the pile. Be sure to have them help spread the compost on your garden in the spring, so they can see the results.

Teach your grandchildren about world geography by hanging a large world map in your home. Every time they visit, let them pick a place in the world that they would like to discover. Visit websites, read books, cook food from that region, write letters to people you know who live there, and draw pictures of the place.

Adopt an overseas soldier with your grandchild and send cards, letters, and packages.

Engage your grandchildren in helping you plan and hold a yard, garage, or jumble sale. They can help you sort through your stuff, set up the sale, and collect payments. At the end, give them a cut of the proceeds. There are lots of great lessons in holding a sale.

Breed butterflies together. Watch them grow from eggs to caterpillars, then from chrysalis to beautiful butterflies, and set them free together. What a wonderful lesson about change, growth, and freedom.

Get your grandchildren involved in a service organization, literacy organization, library, school, or a corporation's reading scheme. They offer rewards and awards, and most importantly encourage reading.

Check online, at the local school, or at the library for suggested reading lists for children your grandchild's age. Read the books on the list, setting an example and giving you and your grandchild something in common to talk about.

Children are little explorers. Their natural curiosity will spur them to venture where no man has gone before... or at least no child. While you want to keep them safe, try not to dampen their enthusiastic curiosity—in fact, nurture it! It will serve them well in life.

Visit websites for grandparents and children with print out activity pages. There's a great selection of them on the Internet, and there are many quick and easy math, art, science, and language learning experiences disguised as fun.

Effective learning takes place through the process of having fun. Why? Because your grandchildren will stick with it and see a task through to the end if it's interesting. Fun learning will keep them motivated and absorbed for hours.

Parlez-vous another language? Teach your grandchildren words and phrases in your second tongue from an early age. The younger they learn, the faster they learn.

Is your grandchild bilingual or learning a new language? Encourage their language development skills by taking some lessons in the language he or she is learning.

Stock up on children's activity books that include stories to read and games to play, which make learning fun. Keep them on hand at your house and when on the go.

Visit a museum that has a "hands-on" exhibit to make history come to life. Being able to dig like an archaeologist, wear clothes from the 17th century, play with toys from long ago, or plant seeds in the manner planters did thousands of years ago, is a lot more engaging than looking at things through a glass window. An interactive activity is an engaging learning experience for your grandchildren.

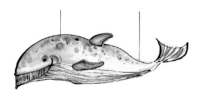

Kids love to achieve goals through multi-level challenges. Have several steps, quizzes, or games of increasing degrees of difficulty, and a final grand prize to really motivate them to learn a new skill.

Having fun when learning is key—for all of us! Learn a new language, hobby, or skill and show your grandchildren how much fun it is. They'll see your enjoyment and will develop a thirst for learning too.

Did you learn the ABC's or other language skills by singing a well-known song? And you still remember it, don't you? That's because the brain functions in a special way with music. If you want your grandkids to remember something, become a composer and set it to music.

Carry a tape measure with you everywhere you go and let your grandchildren measure anything and everything. The car, a rock, the length of your arm—it's a great way to apply math skills.

Do you sew? Teach your grandchildren to sew and they'll learn math skills by measuring fabric, thread, and yarn. They'll learn spatial awareness skills when they place patterns on the fabric, and their dexterity and creativity will get a boost too.

Science isn't just about the periodic table and facts. It's also about exploring the world around us. Be aware of the science around you and point it out to your grandchildren. Teach them about photosynthesis and how it helps plants grow, about the link between gravity and apples falling from a tree, and the effects of chemical reactions when cooking. Encourage them to explore the scientific world at their fingertips.

Is your grandchild interested in a specific sport? Help them learn all about it—from the rules and the techniques to the top players and record-breaking scores. Go to games, visit websites, and read books or magazines about the sport. They'll be gaining valuable learning skills, while also having fun and developing a passion about the sport.

Teach your grandchildren to read maps. Let them guide you to the mall, the campsite, the vacation destination, or around your own backyard.

As your grandchildren learn and grow, it may be hard to keep up with the developmental stages they go through. Get a basic book about the different stages of growth your grandchildren will go through. Talk with their parents about their development from infant to toddler all the way to "tween" and "teen" years. You'll then know what to expect and how to support their progress.

Play chess with your grandchildren. It helps them develop thinking and reasoning skills while playing a cool "retro" game.

Ask your grandchild to be the family reporter, writing short daily articles about what you've been doing while visiting or vacationing as a family. Your budding news anchor can even video record a daily morning update or evening summary of the day.

Ask your grandchildren to research and plan a family vacation or outing. They can present their research findings and proposed plans for the vacation to the family with options to choose from. They'll feel like they have a say in what the family does, and learn great research skills along the way.

Fill a big basket with musical instruments that your grandchildren can use at any time. Not collector's items, just percussion instruments, wooden flutes, and other inexpensive instruments. They'll learn all kinds of good skills, and will also have fun filling the minutes with music.

Help your grandchild improve her spatial awareness skills by drawing a diagram of a room, then planning and rearranging the furniture—all on paper.

Are your grandchildren interested in nature? There are many activities you can do with them to draw out their naturalistic talents—hiking, gardening, visiting animal farms, and researching dinosaurs are just a few.

Some kids are more active and learn more through physical activities. If your grandchild can't sit still, it may be because they require this physical stimulation. Support their learning style with active, hands-on, learning activities, and encourage them to use their bodies to express emotions appropriately.

Learn some basic sign language and teach your grandchildren how to sign with you, so you can have a special form of communication between the two of you.

Watch a TV show or movie with your grandchildren, then discuss what they learned. What was the message? How did the music make them feel? What do they know about the setting? How did they do those special effects? Entertainment can have a learning element too.

Give each one of your grandchildren a camera and ask them to take pictures that tell a story. Print the photos and provide poster boards for them to glue the photos in order and write captions beneath them. You'll have published photographers and authors in your family before you know it.

Your grandchild could be a budding zoologist! Take a camera and a notebook to the zoo and have your grandchild take photos of animals in various positions. Make notes about the position of the tiger's tail as he paces back and forth and watch the way the monkeys carry their young around. Then go to the library and research online to discover why animals exhibit different types of behavior. The photos will give you good reminders of the things you observed together.

There are multiple intelligences, and your grandchild may excel in some more than others. Linguistic, spatial, musical, logical, interpersonal, kinesthetic, and emotional intelligences can all be developed. Reinforce your grandchild's strengths, and encourage them in the areas that are more challenging for them.

Exposure to music can help kids improve their coordination, understand their culture, relax, and even increase their math skills. Introduce music in your day-to-day life with them—in the car, at dinner, during homework, and at naptime. Classical music has been shown to increase brain functions, so don't forget the Beethoven.

Volunteering opens up so many learning opportunities by exposing children to things they might not otherwise experience. Get your grandchildren to collect for a charity and count the money; go to a food bank and help prepare meals; become a mentor to younger children; or plant trees on Arbor Day. Your grandchildren will learn practical skills, as well as develop good character and values.

Fun facts, quizzes, and word games will help your grandchild learn excellent thinking, logic, and analytical skills.

Have a family spelling bee. Once your younger grandchildren start learning to read and write they can participate also, as long as you use appropriate words for each age group. It's all good fun, but make sure it's a little challenging for everyone.

Do you like to learn? Are you aware of learning each and every day? The truth is, we all learn every day of our lives—we never stop. Teach your grandchildren to love learning.

The library is a great place to spend a rainy afternoon with your grandchildren. Most libraries have a children's story hour for younger kids, and older kids will also be able to find books they like, or even use computers.

Sometimes children learn the most by teaching. Ask them to be the teacher. They'll pay attention in a whole different way, and you'll also get an idea of what they know. They can teach you about everything, from using your computer to making macaroni and cheese.

You have many skills you probably take for granted that you can teach your grandchildren. Do you know how to knit or crochet? Get out the needles and yarn and teach your grandchild to make something they can use. They'll gain eye-hand coordination, and following patterns will teach them math skills.

Follow the weather with your grandchild. Learn about cumulous clouds and how rain is made. Study snowflakes and thunderstorms. Weather makes science tangible.

Help your grandchild set up a business. A lemonade stand is a great lesson in product development, marketing, customer service, and finance and budgeting.

Learn about another culture with your grandchildren by building a home common to that culture. Build a Native American teepee or Hogan, an African hut, or even a log cabin.

When you travel with your grandchildren, keep track of the license plates you see, and make a list of fun facts you know about the countries, states, or cities of the cars you come across.

Get a world globe. There are so few of them around these days that your grandchild may never have seen one. It will allow them to get a whole new perspective on the planet.

As your grandchildren get older, they will start to care more about their appearance. Get them some good basic skincare products and teach them how to take care of their skin. Remember that a healthy diet and drinking plenty of water are just as important as washing your face and moisturizing for healthy skin.

Help your grandchildren write a how-to book about something they know. It could be about something as simple as how to tie your shoes or as complicated as how to create a video game. They will learn a lot by putting what they know down in print.

Go fly a kite or paper airplane
with your grandchild! They will
learn about air patterns, gravity,
and wind. Just make sure you
keep hold of little ones if it's
really windy.

*Play "Twenty Questions" with your
grandchildren whenever you have
some time to kill. It will help them
learn at least twenty things about
whatever object or person you choose.*

*Make a boat with your grandchildren. Try it out in
the bathtub first to make sure it floats, then take it
to a stream, river, or lake near you. In the process,
they will learn about floatation, displacement, and
stability, as well as all sorts of great science and
math principles.*

on the go

Visit your childhood home with your grandchildren. Show them the places you used to go and tell them real stories that took place there to spur their imaginations. They will have a glimpse into their own family history and will see you in a whole new light.

Take your grandchildren to the beach and help them build the biggest, most amazing sandcastle they've ever seen. Don't forget to record it for posterity with your camera—before the tide comes in!

Create a scrapbook where you can save the mementos of your travels and adventures with your grandkids. Take the pages to a scrapbook store and make a color copy to send to your grandchildren, so they can enjoy and remember your good times together.

Your local bookstore may have story, music, and play areas for children where you can while away the hours without even having to buy anything.

If you think your grandchild will get bored just traveling with you, ask him to bring a buddy. It will be a great opportunity for your grandchild to show his friend what fun grandparents you are.

There are museums for everything! In addition to the usual art or natural history museums, there are museums devoted to educating the public about fire trucks, medicine, buildings, the postal service, toys, and much more. Check your phone book or your city's website for a listing of local museums.

Take your grandchildren to an art gallery to see an exhibition of a favorite artist. Do a little research together about the artist ahead of time, so you can both really understand the artist's approach and then talk about what you like and dislike about it. They'll love that you made the time to go with them.

You don't have to go away to have fun. Hold a slumber party at your house! Invite your grandchildren over and get out the blankets and sleeping bags. Watch movies, eat popcorn, play games, and stay up late with them. Sleep on the couch if the floor is too hard for you.

Take your grandchildren to visit a nearby horse farm. Get a tour—they'll be fascinated! Learn about the care and feeding of the horses, and finish with a horse ride (or pony ride if they are younger).

Take a train ride with your grandchildren —even a short ride is fun for younger kids. Take the time to watch the trains, examine how they work, talk to a conductor, get a treat at the train station, and take some photos. You may have a train conductor in the family some day.

Do your young grandchildren have a favorite TV show or kiddy musical group? Surprise them with a concert or a seat in the TV audience of their favorite show. It will be an experience they will never forget.

Is there a harbor near you? A dock or mooring is worth a visit to look at the boats, watch the fishermen, and talk about life on the water. Make sure you all dress appropriately if you decide to go on a boat ride—life jackets required.

Older grandchildren may get bored with the usual family activities. Why not give them a break—set them up with a pre-paid card or some tokens for a video or amusement arcade, and let them get some time away from younger siblings. They'll think you are the most cool grandparents in town.

Visit the local fire station. Firefighters are usually quite willing to show the children the fire trucks and engines, where they eat and sleep, and what to do if they are ever in a fire. Just make sure the kids know to cover their ears when the sirens go off.

When was the last time you went to a rock concert? Find out your grandchild's favorite band and get tickets for the two of you. Open your mind and find something you like about your grandchild's music. You'll have a shared experience—and that's what memories are made of. Then switch it. Take your grandchild to a concert of one of your favorites.

Visit a farm with your grandchildren and "pick your own." Apples, berries, peaches, and pumpkins are all tastier when you've gathered or picked them yourself. You can extend the activity by making a yummy pie together when you get home.

Find the best place to watch the sunrise or sunset in your area. Plan an outing with your grandkids, so you can experience the miracle of a sunrise or sunset together, even if it means getting up early. There's something special about the opening and closing of the day.

Take a trip to the flower show. Flowers, both common and unusual, are fascinating to kids, and it can be a great learning experience. Let them pick out a plant to bring home as a special gift from your outing together.

Amusement parks are a favorite family vacation destination. Plan your trip carefully so your energy levels coordinate with your grandchildren's and everyone has fun. Knowing where the long lines are, as well as where there are places to sit and rest, will make a theme park visit more fun for everyone.

Go on a bird watching venture with your grandchildren. Start in your own backyard, then move on to the park, the city, and the countryside. You can even plan a special trip to see endangered birds or awe-inspiring birds of prey.

Is there a building site near you? Take a field trip to see the progress of a new development—children love to watch the bulldozers and cranes. You can also get a DVD of these machines at work that will keep younger children mesmerized for hours!

Visit a fish market with your grandchildren. Go early in the morning when the fish are fresh. Explain how fish are caught and brought to market. You can read a book about fish or look on the Internet together for more information. The sights will be intriguing and the pungent smells will certainly be memorable.

Make a special trip to a bakery near you. Ask the baker if your grandchildren can watch the bread and pastries being made, see the big ovens, and also if they can watch the packaging process. These things are entrancing for children—and a yummy treat to round off the visit will definitely go down well.

Take an afternoon to visit your local plant nursery or garden. Ask to see where the plants grow, how they are transplanted, and how they should be cared for. Your grandchild can take home a small plant to care for as a memento from the visit.

Visit the local recycling center with your grandchildren. They will be enthralled with the sorting, machinery, and processing. You may light a conservationist spark in them that will last a lifetime.

Take a "Habitat for Humanity" family vacation in which all family members work together to build or repair homes for needy families. Families bond and have fun, and the younger generations learn about the ethic of volunteerism.

Collect a pebble or rock from each special outing you go on with your grandchildren. Keep them in a special jar or dish. When they visit, you can go through the rocks and remember all the great places you've been together.

Collect menus, brochures, and even place mats when you travel with your grandchildren. Later on, send them a note written on the back of one telling them how much you loved traveling with them and all the things you enjoyed. They'll feel special getting real mail, and it's a great way to remember the trip.

Children tend to throng to sugar like bees to honey. When you're traveling, set a limit on the amount of sugary goodies your grandkids eat. It might make them happy at the time, but a total sugar rush will make them crash later—and it won't be pretty.

If your younger grandchildren are getting unruly, take them to an adventure playground in your area. Let them channel their excess energy into some positive exercise, rather than destroying your house.

A Science Museum is a great place to visit on a rainy afternoon. Your grandchildren will be fascinated by the great hands-on experiments the museum has to offer. It will definitely become a favorite place for them to visit over and over again.

Gather up the grandchildren and go to a live sporting event. For little ones, it won't matter if it's the local high school baseball game or a major league event. The sites, sounds, scents, and action will all seem marvelous to them. Older kids will love going to support their favorite team.

When traveling with grandchildren, keep in mind that their attention span may not be as long as yours. Take activities with you, like books, paper and crayons, and portable games. These can be lifesavers on long car journeys or during unexpected delays at airports.

Are you bowled over by the sheer magnificence of your grandchildren? How about bowling with them? Bowling is a favorite family sport and a great outing for a half-day or even longer. Most bowling alleys have children's balls, and some can adapt the lanes to be more kid-friendly.

Hiking is a great way to introduce and teach your grandchildren about nature. It's also a fun way to get your grandchildren to exercise. Select trails that are suitable for both you and your grandchildren, starting with short hikes. Work towards a goal, like hiking up a mountain together.

Can't handle a week on the road with the grandkids? Have them stay with you instead, and take a small trip each day to an interesting or fun destination nearby.

You may not have a bicycle built for two, but you can certainly purchase yourself and your grandchildren some cheap second-hand bikes to go exploring on. Cycle around your neighborhood or take your grandchildren for a ride along a scenic bike path. Don't forget the helmets, and make sure you go over the safety rules with your grandchildren ahead of time.

Help your grandchild train for a fun run or walk geared for kids. Elementary children can handle a 3 mile, but there are also even shorter walks or runs. You might find one in a fun destination where you can combine a vacation and mini-marathon for both of you.

Watching a DVD at home is great, but there's something magical about going to the movie theater. Check that your choice of movie is acceptable with mom and dad, and ensure the rating is appropriate for your grandchild's age. You can get movie reviews on parenting websites, so you can gauge the fear levels for little ones and the boredom levels for teenagers. Then sit back, relax, and enjoy a couple of hours of pure entertainment.

Ask your grandchildren for their input as you get ready to go on an adventure with them. If they help you plan the trip, they'll get more excited as they anticipate the escapade.

When you travel with your grandchildren, take a note of their doctors and medical history, as well as any health insurance information. While you don't want to anticipate any problems, you do want to be prepared just in case.

Try exploring a less traveled destination with your grandchildren. Smaller cities usually have less expensive hotel rates, but still have top-notch sites and things to do.

Before heading out, remember the three R's: Research, research, and research! Look for family discounts, vacation packages, holiday recommendations, as well as any other interesting tips you can find out before the trip. You'll save money, time, and headaches.

Plan any trips or outings ahead of time to work around your grandchild's busy schedule—and yours. It may take months to find a time when you are both free for a getaway.

Trips and travel don't have to break your budget. Most children will not remember the money you spend; they'll remember the good times you had together. Plan ahead, don't overbook yourselves, and make it fun. You'll find your grandchildren really don't need all the extras.

Assess your grandchild's and your priorities for any pleasure trip or outing you take together. Accept that your priorities will differ, and come to an agreement ahead of time about where you'll go and what you'll spend time doing. Compromise is a great skill to learn.

As you start to take your grandchildren places, take baby steps first by taking them on small day trips or trips of two or three days. This will get you all used to the idea of embarking on a much longer trip.

When you plan time on the road with grandchildren, think long and hard about their interests. What activities or places of natural beauty would be fun and interesting through their eyes?

Take a learning vacation with your grandchildren. Find a place where you can learn new skills together, like yoga, art, jewelry making, or a new sport. Make sure there's a nice balance of activities and downtime in the schedule for a well-rounded trip.

When you're on the move with young grandchildren, carry a recent photo of each of them with you. If they get lost and you need help finding them, you can become a super sleuth and use the photo as a means of identifying them to people who may have spotted them. It's also a good idea to make sure your grandchildren have their names and your telephone number in their pocket, or an ID bracelet.

Did you know there are travel agencies that specialize in planning grandparent and grandchild travel? Look on the Internet or in your phone book for an agency that has tours and destinations that are friendly for both grandparents and grandkids.

Sailing, sailing over the ocean blue. Take your older grandchildren on a sailing trip. It will not only be a great adventure for them, but it will also teach them how to handle a boat and practice good seamanship.

When you are out and about, enjoy seeing the world through your grandchildren's eyes. It will remind you of how in awe you were of every new experience you had as a child.

Always carry snacks and supplies with you when you travel with your grandchildren. Even a short day trip will require some back-up food. Kids can get grouchy when they are hungry...and so can you. You never know when you'll be in a spot where there aren't refreshments.

Many families love the open sea. There are many child-friendly cruise ship companies that specialize in providing entertainment for little ones and their families.

Road trips are a great way to travel with grandchildren. There's more room for flexibility when you have your own wheels, and you can fit a whole lot more "just in case" items in a car than you can in a suitcase.

Get out the tents and sleeping bags and go camping or caravanning. Even if you camp in your own backyard, it will be an out of the ordinary event that your grandchildren will remember for a long time.

Offer to help your grandchildren pack before a trip, or help their parents if they are pressed for time. This way you can ensure they'll have everything they need for the adventure you have in mind.

Make a generic packing list that you can use as a basis for any outing with grandchildren. There will be essentials that you'll always need, regardless of whether it's a trip to the snowy mountains or the beach. You can add to the list according to your specific destination each time.

It's nice for grandchildren to get one-on-one time with grandma and grandpa. Plan a special trip for each grandchild. Each child will feel special getting your undivided attention, and it will help you get to know your grandchild.

Festivals and fairs are fun to visit with grandchildren because you never know what you will find there. Livestock exhibits are appealing to children who love animals; while others can't wait to see those big machines at the tractor pull contests! If your grandchildren are more creative, they may prefer to wander around the arts and crafts stalls.

When you travel with your grandchildren, make sure you know where to find an Internet café or access to wireless Internet connection. You can find the Internet in the remotest places, so it should be easy to touch base with mom and dad or other family members. If you have grand-teens, they will definitely want to check for emails from their friends while they are away.

Teenage grandchildren will begin to want more time doing the things they enjoy and less time in "family activities." Ask them what they'd like to do, and allow them short periods of time on their own. Be sure their parents are comfortable with this approach, and schedule times and places to meet up again. They'll be more willing to join the family after doing something more to their liking.

The theater, the theater…. Many children never have opportunities to see live theater performances. Take your grandchild to see a live play or musical. Turn it into a special afternoon treat and go to lunch or tea. For younger grandchildren, see a performance that is geared toward their age group. Older grandchildren will enjoy the same theater experiences you do!

Always travel with a first aid kit with lots of extra bandages for young grandchildren.

When you visit a theme or amusement park with grandchildren, always know where the first aid station, information stands, and restrooms are located. Agree to a meeting place in case you get separated, and bring dry clothes if you plan to ride the water rides.

family matters

As a grandparent, you and your grandchild's parents are learning together—every new baby is a new road, and you are there to support each other along the way.

Your family is a melting pot of viewpoints, experiences, personalities, and lifestyles, and you as a grandparent are the connector that brings your amazing family together on common ground.

Tread gently when you talk with your children about your grandchildren. Always remember that they are the parents and you'll have a better relationship with them and your grandchildren if you respect their choices.

Compliment your grandchild's parents about their parenting efforts. You'll boost their confidence, and confident parents are better parents.

Tell your grandchildren about your parents, so they will know how important they were to you and have a sense of the generations that came before them. And remember, a picture speaks a thousand words.

Do you like unsolicited advice? If not, then maybe you can understand why your grandchildren's parents might not like it either. Sometimes it's best to be asked before you offer your opinion.

Listen to your children when they need to talk about parenting and your grandchildren. Your role is not to judge, it is to love and support.

Discipline is often a bone of contention between parents and grandparents. Honest and open communication about parents' choices around rules and punishments, and grandparents' ability and willingness to enforce those methods, can prevent misunderstandings and family arguments.

Be a good family connector for all your grandchildren. Bring cousins together as frequently as you can, so they really get to know each other. They'll develop a larger sense of family and a circle of love they'll have for the rest of their lives.

Savor the anticipation of your grandchild's arrival. Put a copy of the baby's sonogram on your refrigerator with a magnet. You'll have plenty of photos of them through the years, but for many grandparents nothing will ever compare to that first sonogram.

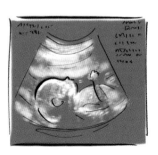

Mark important dates for your grandchildren on your calendar. Football games, dance recitals, school tests, plays, and concerts can be very important to them, and they'll know that you are interested in their lives. Call to wish them good-luck, and ask about how it went afterwards. You can be their best cheerleader.

When it comes to disagreements between grandparents and parents, focus on what is in the best interest of the grandchild.

Tell your grandchildren stories about their parents. Kids love this, especially the funny things their parents did or said when they were younger. Be sure to consider whether or not their parents will be OK with the stories you are sharing.

Make up a quiz about yourself for your grandchildren to take. Do they know where you were born? Where you went to school? The name of your pets when you were young? How old you were when you got married? They'll learn about you and their family history in a fun and interesting way.

Ever thought about writing your memoirs? Do it!
Get down on paper the key experiences in your life,
what you've learned, the work you've done, and the
people you've known. There are books and websites
devoted to memoir writing that are a great source to
guide you. The generations to come will be grateful
that you took the time to record your family history.

*Have some old home movies and
slides in the closet? Dig them out
and transfer them to DVD. A family
home movie night will bring back
memories, and the grandchildren
will get a big kick out of seeing you
younger in out-of-fashion clothes!*

Want some family interaction? Bring out the cards and board games. They don't have to be complicated games to get the competition and laughter going, and you'll find that different generations will relate to each other in the process.

Tell your grandchildren funny stories about yourself when you were growing up, especially the embarrassing ones. It will convey the message that everyone in their family has gone through awkward times and they will too. But you all live to laugh about them together later.

Pets are part of the family, too. If you have cats, dogs, birds, or other pets, get your grandkids to feed and care for them. They'll learn the importance of being responsible pet-owners.

Gather your family together on a regular basis. Even if some family members can't be there, the ritual of gathering as a family will be remembered fondly by your grandchildren in years to come, and hopefully they'll carry on the tradition themselves.

Make a phone call just to your grandchild. They'll feel special that you called just to talk to them. If they don't feel like talking, don't take it personally—some kids are just not phone people. Either way, they'll know you called and that you care. They'll notice even more if you DON'T call!

Offer to help your grandchildren's parents with their busy schedules. Can you make the Halloween costumes? Maybe it would be helpful if they gave you their grocery-shopping list one week? Parents with more than one child may have trouble attending school programs if they are scheduled at the same time—filling in for them might be a huge help.

Give your grandchildren self-addressed stamped envelops and note paper. Ask them to send you a note or drawing once a month, and enlist their parents to help out. It will be fun for younger children to have something to mail, and you'll love the surprises you get from time to time!

Sometimes it seems that families only connect around problems. Take time to share the good news in your life with your children and grandchildren. The small pleasures; the triumphs and accomplishments, bring positive energy to your family relationships.

Make sure your grandchildren are aware of their cultural and ethnic backgrounds. Tell them stories, visit the places that are significant to your culture, read books, and play games that reinforce their connection to their ancestors. Make it fun and they will be more eager to learn.

Make friends with your "co-grandparents." Often grandparents on one side of the family try to compete with the other side of the family for their grandchildren's love and attention. You'll be better off in the long run if you are on the same team.

Divorce is a fact of life in many families and can be confusing for grandchildren. Make sure they know it's not their fault if grandma and grandpa get divorced. Assure them that they are loved and will still have special time with each grandparent.

If your grandchildren are being raised in a different religion from yours, take time to learn about it and look for the similarities with yours, so you can focus on the things you have in common.

If your grandchildren's parents go through a divorce, try to remain as neutral as possible. It doesn't do your grandchildren any good to hear you speak badly about their parents, and your interest should be in what is best for your grandchildren.

When divorce occurs in your family, you can help your grandchildren by reassuring them that it was not their fault. Be a listening ear for grandchildren, so they know you are a safe person for them to talk to about the divorce without any judgments.

If you are divorced, try to set aside your differences with your former spouse and have family time together for the sake of your grandchildren. They will feel more secure knowing some things are still constant in their lives.

While we'd all love our families to be perfect, the reality is that difficult family relationships and hurtful situations do sometimes happen. Take the high road—be the grandparent who doesn't choose sides and whose focus is on your grandchildren. You'll be better off in the long run, and so will your grandchildren.

If a negative family situation has caused you to have trouble seeing your grandchildren, continue to send cards and letters to them on a regular basis, and keep copies of them in case they are not delivered to your grandchild. One day you may have the opportunity to share those copies with them, and they will know that you cared all along.

If your child has married someone you don't approve of, don't cut yourself off from your grandchildren by refusing to accept that parent. What are your priorities? Do you want to be right, or do you want to have a close, loving, and supportive relationship with your grandchildren?

Family reunions are a great way to bring all generations together at one time. If your family doesn't have a standing annual family reunion, why not take the lead and start one?

Family reunions can be as simple as an afternoon potluck picnic or as elaborate as a family cruise. Just make sure it's fun for family of all ages, and your grandchildren will look forward to the reunion every year.

Having some difficulty with disciplining your grandchildren? Reinforce their positive behaviors. You can create a behavior chart and reward them with good marks or stickers when they've behaved. Always consult their parents first before you try any discipline techniques.

If you have strained family relationships and aren't seeing your grandchild as much as you'd like, family mediation with a qualified professional may be an option. Creating an agreement for visitation through mediation is less adversarial and less costly than a court battle.

If you are a primary caregiver for some grandchildren, or even just spending more time with them than others, try to have quality one-on-one time with your other grandchildren. They may feel like they are cheated and don't get as much of your attention and love.

Take the step today to break the cycle of negative relationships in your family. Reach out to an estranged family member, and if you owe them an apology, do it. Forgive and forget and move on. You can set the example of family healing.

If you are a step-grandparent, make it clear that you are not trying to replace your grandchildren's "biological" grandmother or grandfather. You can have a very special role in their lives, but may need to take a back seat now and then, and that's OK.

When you're caregiving for grandchildren, make sure you have the ability to take them for emergency medical care if they get injured or get very sick. Find out from their parents which doctor and hospital they prefer, and if you need to show proof of health insurance or have special legal authority to approve health care treatment.

Let go of, "when I was raising children I did it THIS way." That was then; this is now. The choices your children make about disciplining, dressing, and raising your grandchildren may not be up to your personal standards, but learn to embrace the fact that "different" isn't synonymous with "bad."

Do your grandchildren have health insurance? If not, find out how you can get coverage for them, either through a private policy or a public program. And familiarize yourself with what doctor visits, medicines, and equipment the insurance covers.

If your family has a rough time with family gatherings, discuss ahead of time, and set some ground rules. You may need to agree to no or limited alcohol consumption. Some discussion topics may be taboo if they lead to arguments or alienation of some family members. You may even want to set a time limit on the gathering. Whatever happens, try to focus on the positive aspects of family togetherness.

Many grandparents take on the responsibility of raising their grandchildren full-time due to problems their parents are experiencing. If you step in to raise grandchildren, make sure everything is covered legally in terms of custody or guardianship. You need to do things by the law to ensure your grandchildren are kept safe.

Make sure your grandchildren are going for regular "well child" doctor visits to check their growth. They'll need certain immunizations periodically, and the doctor will make sure their growth and health are right on target.

If you are care giving for your grandchildren, you may need to register them for school. Ask the school what information you'll need to provide to register them, including health records, birth certificate, and possibly a parent's signature.

When you are a primary caregiver for your grandchildren, the relationship with their parents can be complicated. Try to have an agreement with their parents, setting out clear boundaries and roles in regard to the children. It will make life easier for everyone involved.

If you are raising your grandchildren full-time, it will be helpful for you to talk with other grandparents who are going through the same joys and challenges. Anyone can empathize and support you, but only someone who has walked a mile in your moccasins will really know how you feel. Find a grandparent support group—or start one yourself!

Often when grandparents take on the role of primary caregiver, they miss being the traditional grandparent who spoils their grandchildren with treats and then sends them home at the end of the day. Take a break from being the disciplinarian, and do the fun things you'd do if you weren't raising them. It's an important part of your relationship.

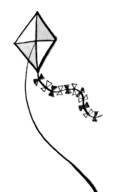

If you're a caregiver for your grandchildren, be sure to take time out for yourself. Making sure that you are mentally and physically healthy should be a top priority for you—you can't care for them if you aren't in top shape yourself.

When you are care giving for grandchildren, communication with other family members is vital. Talk about why you are care giving, how you feel about it, and how other family members can support you.

Caring for grandchildren can be a joyful as well as a stressful experience. Take a break and be good to yourself now and then. Looking after kids can be draining and you need to conserve your energy.

There are many great online resources for grandparents who care for grandchildren, whether you are babysitting, providing regular childcare, or raising them full-time. Look out for online support groups, discussion boards, and chat rooms, as well as articles, advice columns, financial planning tools, and more.

If you're a grandparent who provides child care on a regular basis, it's a good idea to have a child-care agreement that spells out your role, including rules the parents want to enforce, discipline preferences, how expenses like food will be handled, etc. It's best to get these things in writing, so the boundaries are clear to everyone involved.

To pay or not to pay? That is the question. Many grandparents are paid for providing childcare on a regular basis. Whether your grandchild's parents pay you or not, be sure you all agree ahead of time so there are no misunderstandings.

It can sometimes be hard to keep up with demands of your grandchildren. Let them know that sometimes you need help too. It's OK to let them know that you are also vulnerable now and then.

The more time you spend with your grandchildren—whether as a primary caregiver or child-care provider—the more you will play a role in their lives. Your influence is strong, so always be on your best behavior.

Are you caring for a grandchild with special needs? There are support organizations out there that can help you with a range of issues, from attention disorders and physical disabilities to psychological and emotional disorders, and many others. Check your phone book or the Internet for organizations, and look into the support they have to offer. Educate yourself—you are your grandchild's advocate.

Sometimes children with learning disabilities or other special needs may have trouble building relationships with other children. Seek advice from a professional counselor, or get them into a group for children with similar disabilities, so they know they are not alone.

It takes a whole family to raise a child. If you're playing a more prominent role in your grandkid's lives, don't hesitate to call upon extended family—aunts, uncles, and cousins—for support.

If you have stepped in as a surrogate parent to your grandchildren, you might have friends who are willing to spend time with them, especially if their grandchildren live far away. It will give you a break and give your grandchildren another loving adult in their lives. In return, your friend will enjoy having fun with your grandchildren.

If your grandchild has a disability, the most important thing you can do is see the whole child and not just the disability. Your grandchild needs to feel your love and acceptance. You don't want to be in denial about the disability, but it doesn't have to overshadow everything you do together.

If you are raising grandchildren full-time, be sure to have a legal plan in place in case anything should happen to you. You'll want to be sure your grandchild has a safe and secure future.

If your grandchildren have been abused or neglected, they may need extra loving care and patience. Time and love will heal wounds, but you will both need counseling and the help of supportive services.

With today's complicated families, children can end up with more than the usual four grandparents. You can be a grandparent angel by helping to coordinate visits and family gatherings with the other grandparents and facilitate relationships among them. Make friends, not enemies!

As your grandchildren grow into young adults, you may not always agree with their life choices. Examine your choices. You can either be the person in their lives who disapproves, judges, and isolates, or you can be the person they talk to openly about their choices. It's important you accept them for who they are. Which is it for you?

When you give a grandchild a financial gift of any kind, it's a good idea to also give them a small fun gift at the same time. Something they can immediately enjoy.

Give the gift of music. Talk it over with your grandchildren's parents, and offer to pay for piano, violin, drum, or voice coaching lessons. It's an extra that many parents can't afford, and it will enrich your grandchildren's lives.

Give your grandchildren phone calling cards, or minutes on their mobile phones, so you can call or text message each other. The more frequent your contact with them, the more you'll really get to know each other. And teenagers do love their phones!

Does your grandchild have a savings account? If not, check with their parents to be sure they're OK with it, and open one. Seed the account with an initial gift, and add some to it on a regular basis, or on birthdays or holidays. When your grandchild grows up, it will be a wonderful gift to have a nest egg that will help them with education, their first car, or living expenses.

Teach your grandchildren how to save by helping them create both short-term goals (saving for a toy or ice cream) and long-term goals (saving for a bike, an expensive video game, computer, or college). Give them the opportunity to earn money through chores, and divide up their earnings between spending, short-term, and long-term savings.

Give a grandchild a subscription to their favorite magazine as a gift. They'll get something they really want, and will be reminded of your gift every month for a year!

Help your grandchildren learn about charitable giving. Take four jars and label them "Giving," "Spending," "Short-term Savings," and "Long-term Savings." Coach them to put equal amounts into each jar whenever they earn or are gifted money. When they have a bit of money built up, help them choose what cause they'd like to donate their giving money to according to their interests.

Make your grandchild an audio or DVD of bedtime stories. Hearing your voice as a part of their bedtime ritual each night will help make you a familiar and special person in their lives.

Check in with your grandchildren's parents to find out how you can help pay for some of the extras, like school field trips, birthday parties, allowance, tutoring, or a new winter coat. They'll appreciate you consulting them before offering support.

Give your grandchildren opportunities to earn money. Whether they earn a quarter for helping you take out the trash, or $100 for helping you run a yard sale, it will teach them that hard work is the way to earn money. Check with their parents first to make sure they agree with your approach.

Take out a life insurance policy with your grandchildren as beneficiaries.

A Savings Bond makes a great gift for grandchildren. They may not understand it now, but in the future they will be pleasantly surprised when they have money for college or their first big purchase.

Start a college account for your grandchildren. There are special savings accounts, in-state university programs, and even business-based accounts that will donate money to your grandchild's saving account every time you make a purchase. Find out what is available in your area and start saving.

Some parents may limit the gifts you can give your grandchildren. If you want to give your grandchildren more than is acceptable, create a savings account for each grandchild and make deposits instead of giving gifts. When your grandchildren are older and more independent you can give them what you've saved.

Keep the change! Teach your grandchildren to put change from purchases right into their savings accounts. You can do the same. Remember you are a role model for those little minds!

Keep a penny jar. Every time you think of your grandchild, put a penny in the jar. Each night empty your pockets into the jar. Keep your eyes open for coins on the ground when you are walking. When the jar is full, take it to the bank and make a deposit in a savings account for your grandchild. You'll be surprised how quickly coins add up.

Consider giving your grandchildren the meaningful gift of a donation to a "micro credit" business. You can give an animal in their name that will help sustain a family in need in another country.

Help your grandchildren learn about money by getting them to start their own business. Do they have special talents? Little artists can make greeting cards; salespersons can have a lemonade stand; nature lovers can mow lawns; animal lovers can walk dogs. Help them create goals, plan, budget, spend, and save the big money they make.

Next time you go out for dinner with your grandchildren, have them calculate the tip for the waiter.

The most important gift you will ever give your grandchildren doesn't come in a box or package. It can't be wrapped in pretty paper. Your greatest gift is your time, attention, and love. That's what they really need.

Plant a tree in your grandchild's name. The two of you can watch "their" tree grow over the years, and it will be making a positive contribution to the environment.

Financial troubles in your family may lead to you playing a bigger role in your grandchildren's lives. Be diplomatic and sensitive if you help out with expenses. Sometimes it might be nice for your children to believe the money or gifts are coming to them from their parents, not you. The bottom line is that grandchildren get what they need.

Allow your grandchildren to make mistakes with money. Mistakes are really just learning experiences in disguise.

Next time you go on an outing with your grandchildren, give them a budget. Provide a reasonable amount of spending money, and help them think ahead about what they might like to do with it. Teach them to stay within their budget and how to make good spending choices.

Discuss with your grandchildren's parents how much they want their children to know about family finances. Respect their wishes. If they don't want your grandchildren to worry about financial struggles, don't mention them around the children.

Put yourself on a holiday shopping budget when buying gifts for grandchildren. It's easy to go overboard and either overload them with more gifts than they can appreciate or overload your bank account.

It is OK to say "no" to grandchildren. No to gifts you can't afford or that aren't age-appropriate, and no to things they are not allowed to have. They'll get over it. Boundaries are a good thing when they are clear and not overly rigid.

Why not send your grandchild a plane or train ticket as a birthday present, so he or she can come and visit you? The trip doesn't have to take place on a birthday; it will usually take some planning to juggle your schedules.

Sometimes it will seem like the older your grandchild get, the more expensive they are. As they move from small toys and books into the electronic age, their gift expectations may not fit with your budget. Just because your grandchildren want expensive gifts, don't feel that's the only thing you can get them. Ask them for a list of less expensive gift ideas.

Coordinate with your grandchildren's parents when it comes to college savings funds. If they have already started one, it might be better to do it together. Make sure you consult your financial advisor, because there may be situations in which you're better off saving separately.

If your children are struggling financially, be sensitive about giving grandchildren gifts that their parents can't afford. Talk with their parents first about the gift you are giving.

Gifts are about receiving as well as giving. Be a graceful recipient of whatever your children and grandchildren choose to give you. You'll be an excellent example of gracious living for all of them.

Children grow fast and clothes are always needed. Check sizes and style and color preferences with your grandchildren's parents before you buy that bright yellow XL shirt for your size Small grandson!

Your grandchildren will feel more secure if they know that you have a plan to address any financial or work troubles you or your children are facing. They don't need all the details, just the basics will do.

In tough financial times, remember that children absorb everything. Even if you don't think you're discussing financial or work struggles in front of them, they are probably more aware of issues than you realize. Be upfront with them, but don't burden them with too much. Just tell them enough to ease any fears they may have.

Have a holiday gift-making party with your grandchildren. Everyone loves handmade gifts, and their parents will be grateful for a break to go and do their own holiday shopping.

Watch what you say. Children often take things quite literally. If you say their new outfit cost a fortune, they'll believe you and feel guilty about it.

Money is a sensitive topic in any family. The choices your children make about expenditures for your grandchildren may not always be the ones you'd make. Try not to criticize—it's not worth it when things are beyond your control. Offering your opinion when asked is fine, but if you're overly critical it will filter down to your grandchildren and nobody will benefit from your advice.

In rough financial times, your grandchildren just need to know that their basic needs will be met. Reassure them that they'll have a roof over their heads, food to eat, and adequate clothing to wear.

Consider giving your grandchildren the gift of experiences, rather than things. They'll eventually forget the things, but they'll remember the experiences and the skills they acquired for a lifetime.

Remember good old-fashioned layaway when it comes to gifts for grandchildren. Get a gift list in plenty of time, so you can make payments and have those highly desired gifts for your grandchildren at just the right moment.

Are your children promising your grandchildren that you'll give them things without consulting you first? Have a talk with your children and ask them not to commit you to gifts you may not be able or willing to provide. If they need your help with a gift, they should feel free to ask you about it. No one should set your grandchildren up for disappointment.

Get your grandchild a special bank for their money—one that has separate sections for saving, giving, spending, and investing. They'll develop good money habits from a young age that will serve them all their lives.

Consider sharing the cost of high-priced gifts your grandchildren want. You can cost-share with their parents, or help your grandchildren find ways to earn money themselves to help share the costs.

Give grandchildren the gift of travel. Broaden their horizons by taking them to places they've never gone before.

Teach your grandchildren that kindness is the greatest gift of all, especially when it comes to friends. Being a good friend is worth more than any expensive gift they could give a buddy.

When buying gifts for grandchildren, keep the parents in mind. They may never forgive you if you buy your grandchild a drum set that will percussively fill their lives with constant loud drumming.

If your grandchildren get everything they want as soon as they want it, how will they ever learn to plan, anticipate, and really appreciate things?

Make sure your grandchildren know that you don't measure love by the number and cost of gifts received. Love is intangible and always there, no matter what gifts you have to offer.

It's such a challenge to know what gifts your grandchildren will like. Consider giving them a store gift card or certificates, so they can choose their own gifts. Make an outing of it by going with them to spend the gift cards. Even little ones will love the one-on-one attention, and it's fun for them to actually have money to spend.

Hold yourself back when it comes to presents for very young children. They really aren't that interested in all the presents they get— you'll often find they're more interested in playing with the wrapping paper.

Give your grandchild a gift that is an investment in the future. Every year, give them collectible coins directly from the mint. They'll have a wonderful collection that they can enjoy or cash in someday for a big purchase or college education.

As grandchildren get older, a check could be their favorite gift of all. They may be saving up for the latest gadget, a holiday, a car, or another big purchase, in which case your money will go a long way. It could be that they just need the extra cash to do a big grocery shop or update a tired wardrobe. Either way, they will appreciate the cash injection.

Older grandchildren will be thrilled with a gift card from a gasoline or petrol station. They may not have a lot of cash, but they "gotta have" their wheels.

Movie tickets are a great gift for the whole family. They can be used on their own, or you might want to plan a family outing to the movie theater!

Many toys and books have age guidelines on the packaging. Check for these guidelines, so you buy age-appropriate gifts for your grandchildren. Sometimes a toy you think is perfect for your grandchild is actually meant for a much older child and may not be safe.

Games are a great gift for your grandchildren. Find the right games for their ages and abilities. Board games that the family can play together are a great investment in family bonding.

Sports lessons and camps can be pricey and hard for parents to pay for. Give your grandchildren active gifts, such as golf lessons, a summer at football camp, or for the more adventurous, a rock climbing course.

Give your grandchildren a scrapbook that highlights all the special times you've had together. It's a gift they'll have the rest of their lives, while other "things" you give them will be long forgotten once the next new toy fad comes along.

When your grandchildren are young, it may be hard for siblings to watch the birthday child open all those wonderful presents. It's a nice idea to bring a small item for the non-birthday sibling to open, if parents agree.

Once you give a gift to your grandchild it's theirs. What they do with it after that is their business.

If your grandchildren's parents agree, offer to help the little ones go through their toys, games, dolls, and stuffed animals. Help them donate the items that they don't play with anymore to children who don't have toys.

Help your grandchildren write thank-you notes to friends and family after their birthday or a holiday. They'll learn good manners and appreciate the presents they receive.

An afternoon with a grandparent is a wonderful present. Take your grandchild out for lunch and a movie, for a visit to a museum and tea, or even for a hotdog at a ball game. It's these special treats that your grandchild will like best of all.

Give your grandchildren the gift of community spirit and create a holiday gift basket for a needy family. They will learn that giving is far more important than receiving.

All grandparents want to spoil their grandkids, but take a step back and think about the values you are teaching them as they grow up. Spoiled, demanding children grow into self-centered, difficult adults.

Your young grandchildren—and their parents—have certain restaurants they love to frequent. Your children will appreciate gift cards to those restaurants when they are tight on money, and your grandchildren will love tucking into their favorite food as a special treat.

Teach your grandchildren the value of money. Set realistic limits.

Known for her expertise on family issues, Amy Goyer is senior vice president of outreach for Grandparents.com and a columnist for AARP.org. A recognized media authority, her 25 years of experience in intergenerational matters has ranged from local to international and includes a special emphasis on grandparenting.

An Hachette UK Company
First published in Great Britain in 2009 by
Spruce, a division of Octopus Publishing Group Ltd
2–4 Heron Quays, London E14 4JP.
www.octopusbooks.co.uk
www.octopusbooksusa.com

Distributed in the U.S. and Canada for Octopus Books USA
c/- Hachette Book Group USA
237 Park Avenue
New York NY 10017.

978-1-84601-324-9
1-84601-324-0

A CIP catalog record of this book is available from the Library of Congress.

Printed and bound in China
10 9 8 7 6 5 4 3 2 1